Being Billy

Story by Dianne Wolfer

Illustrations by Meredith Thomas

Rigby PM Plus Chapter Books
part of the Rigby PM Program
Sapphire Level

Published by Harcourt Achieve Inc.
10801 N. MoPac Expressway
Building #3
Austin, TX 78759
www.harcourtachieve.com

First published in 2003 by Thomson Learning Australia
Text © Dianne Wolfer 2003
Illustrations © Thomson Learning Australia 2003

10 9 8 7 6 5 4 3 2
07 06 05

Printed and bound in China by 1010 Printing Limited

Being Billy
ISBN 0 75786 926 2

Contents

Chapter 1
Billy and Andrew

Billy loved his big brother Andrew. No one else in the world was as clever and wonderful. When they were together, Billy forgot that he was different.

Billy and Andrew did exciting things together. Things like building forts and catching fish. But what he liked most was putting on plays with Andrew and his friend, Gino. Throughout summer vacation, the three of them made costumes and props, and performed shows for their parents or Gino's dog, Bluey.

Usually, Billy looked forward to the end of summer vacation. He liked shopping for the new school year. This year there was more to buy because Andrew was going to a new school.

"I wish I could go to high school with you," Billy said. "I'll have no one to sit with on the bus. Gino will be on your bus to high school, too. It won't be the same."

"Don't worry. Only another year, then you'll be at high school, too. Besides, you can help with the school play this year. Mrs. Robinson always needs people to help backstage."

"Maybe I could have the lead role."

Andrew smiled. "Maybe."

That was in August. Since then Andrew had made new friends at high school and everything had changed. He went to the movies or the mall all the time, and never invited Billy.

Sometimes Mom made him take Billy, but Andrew's high school friends always stared at him and ignored him. That made Billy mad. Just because he wasn't the same as them didn't mean they could treat him that way.

Billy felt lonely. The kids at his school were usually friendly, but he'd never had a best friend. That was one of the problems when you were different.

Chapter 2
Billy on His Own

The winter holidays came and went. Sometimes Gino and Billy got together, but it wasn't as much fun without Andrew.

Things became steadily worse. When Andrew and Billy went to the supermarket, Andrew refused to give Billy rides in the cart. "We're too old for that, Billy," he said. When Billy tried to hold hands, Andrew pulled away. "Only little kids do that," he said. "Besides, your palms are all sweaty!" Billy wiped his hands on his jeans. Andrew had never complained about his palms before.

Billy watched Andrew. He studied his brother, looking for a sign that he was back to his old self. But all Andrew wanted was to be left alone. Billy tried leaving hints. He left their best costumes on Andrew's bed, but Andrew pushed them away. He left their photo album open to his favorite page — the picture of Bluey standing on their best fort — but Andrew ignored it.

Billy kept trying to get Andrew's attention. One day Andrew did notice.

"Stop sneaking around after me," Andrew shouted. "I'm sick of you staring at me all the time. Why can't you just leave me alone?"

Billy knew Andrew had had enough of him. There's no point crying over spilled milk, their mother always said. So Billy decided he'd have to find something fun he could do on his own. When Mrs. Robinson announced the upcoming school play, the timing seemed perfect.

"We'll be performing 'Midnite.' It's an olden-day story about a cowboy and his pals. Here is a list of the characters. We'll read the play after lunch. Rehearsals will be held after school if you want to try out for a part. We'll also need people to help with costumes, painting sets, lighting, and stage props. I want everyone to be involved!'

Billy looked at the list of characters and Sally helped him read them. Sally sat beside him in class.

"I'm going to try out for the part of the cat," she said. "Do you want to act or have a job backstage?" Billy smiled. Most people would expect him to take an easy job, but Sally never assumed he couldn't do things. Billy remembered acting in plays throughout the summer with Gino and Andrew.

"I want to act," he whispered. "Good for you," Sally replied. "Who do you want to be?" "Someone important!" Billy said.

"What about the lead role, Captain Midnite?"

"Perfect," Billy answered, turning his head dramatically. They giggled until Mrs. Robinson told them to be quiet.

Chapter 3

Rehearsing

"Have you heard Billy's news?" their mother asked Andrew.

Andrew sighed.

Their mother gave him a firm look. "Your brother has landed the main role in the school play."

"You're joking? As if they'd give it to him!" Andrew replied nastily.

"Andrew, you may not have noticed, but your brother is actually a very talented actor."

Andrew snorted. "He'll just make a fool of himself. And us!"

The back door banged and Andrew looked up. His brother was staring at him — a look of disbelief and betrayal on his face.

"It's not often that I'm ashamed of you, Andrew," their mother said quietly, "but I am today. The main reason Billy auditioned was to impress you."

Andrew scowled and went to his room. Stupid play, he thought. He sat on the bed sorting his baseball cards. "Someone has to tell the truth," he muttered.

Billy stopped following Andrew around. At first Andrew was relieved, but after a while he felt guilty. He offered to help Billy learn his lines. If Billy was determined to act in public, at least he could try to minimize the damage.

"That's okay," Billy said. "Mrs. Robinson and Mom are helping. Besides, I already know most of the words."

Andrew put away his baseball cards. He picked up their photo album and opened it to the picture of Bluey on their fort. "He'll soon forget what I said," Andrew told himself. "Billy never holds grudges."

Billy became busy with rehearsals. He loved pretending to be a cowboy, especially when his pals got to chase others.

"Stand and deliver!" they shouted and Billy knew his voice was the loudest.

Mrs. Robinson spent time working with him. She taught Billy when to overact dramatically for laughs, and when to understate his lines for quiet impact. Her patience encouraged Billy to experiment. Soon he was able to help the other kids when they forgot their lines.

Unfortunately, Sally wasn't chosen for the role of the cat. Mrs. Robinson said she could be Dora, the cow. But Sally didn't want to be a cow, so she became an officer.

During Act One, she had to chase Billy across the stage. Sometimes, during lunchtime, Sally and her friends practiced that scene, and then let Billy hang around until the bell rang. Even though he missed the bus ride with Andrew, this was the happiest Billy had ever been at school.

Chapter 4
Stealing the Show

The days before the play whizzed by. Billy started to get nervous. Andrew's words kept playing in his mind.

"Do *you* think I'll make a fool of myself?" he asked Mom one evening.

Mom hugged him. "Of course not. Mrs. Robinson is proud of you. She said this play will be the best she's ever produced!"

"But Andrew still thinks I'll embarrass us, doesn't he?"

Mom hesitated. "Anything we do embarrasses Andrew at the moment," she sighed. "Don't worry. He'll be fine."

Mom turned off the light, but Billy lay awake in the dark. He wanted Andrew to enjoy the play and not be embarrassed that Captain Midnite was his brother.

★　★　★

As soon as he pulled on his costume, Billy's nerves disappeared. His cowboy hat, checked shirt, and cowboy boots made him feel special, but it was the eye mask that Billy really loved. When he wore it, he looked like the other kids.

Billy grinned at the cat, Red Ned, and the rest of his pals. They walked onto the stage and Billy "became" his character. As he rode through Hidden Valley, Billy felt the wind in his hair. When Captain Midnite shook hands with Officer O'Grady, Billy felt their friendship. And when Captain Midnite fell in love with Miss Laura Wellborn, Billy felt his cheeks blush.

Then it was over. The audience cheered and Billy scanned the crowd for Andrew. Andrew was clapping, but the blinding spotlight made it hard for Billy to see his brother's face. They ran offstage. Then the audience stood, cheering even more loudly.

"Go back and bow again," Mrs. Robinson whispered.

They ran back and bowed. Then Mrs. Robinson walked out and she bowed, too.

Mrs. Robinson pretended not to notice the boy offstage who was balancing a huge bouquet of flowers, until he stumbled out to present them to her. The audience cheered again.

"Andrew, can you go backstage and find Billy?" Mom asked. "I have to talk to Mr. Malouf about Billy's sports program."

Billy this, Billy that, Andrew thought. How come it's always Billy that gets the attention? He scuffed his feet, amazed that his brother had done so well.

Things were busy backstage, and Billy was in the midst of it.

"Great job!" Mrs. Robinson praised as she whispered in Billy's ear. A tall man beside her coughed. "Oh, that's right," she said. "Billy, I want to introduce you to Mr. Fox. He works for Channel 5 TV. He'd like to talk to you."

Andrew perked up his ears. Mr. Fox held out his hand and Billy shook it up and down energetically. Andrew looked away in embarrassment. Why did Billy always have to get so excited?

"Great performance, Billy," Mr. Fox said. Billy beamed proudly. "Do you know the show *Here and There*?" Mr. Fox continued.

"Do I know it?" Billy shouted. "I watch it every night! Actually I'm in love with Kylie Minnow!" he whispered.

Andrew rolled his eyes.

"You and every other boy," Mr. Fox laughed. "Well, Billy, I was very impressed with your performance tonight. My niece Sally was . . . "

"I know Sally," Billy interrupted. "She's an officer."

"Yes, she is. Anyway, Billy, I'm glad I came to watch Sally. You see, we've been looking for someone like you to play a new character on *Here and There*. We need a twelve-year-old boy to play Kylie's brother."

Billy shook his head. "But Kylie doesn't have a brother."

"Ah, that's what everyone thinks! He's been living in the country with Kylie's grandma. Soon he'll be moving to Winter Creek to go to high school."

"I'll be twelve next month," Billy remarked.

"Yes," Mr. Fox said with a smile. "Mrs. Robinson told me."

Mr. Fox then spoke to Mom and arranged an interview and screen test. Then Mr. Fox called and asked them to come back for another meeting.

"Billy's a natural," he said. "The screen test was excellent. Billy is exactly what we've been looking for. We want to offer him a contract."

Chapter 5

Here and There

Soon after the play, Billy was being picked up by a Channel 5 driver and taken to the set of *Here and There*. School even let him take time off for filming!

When Billy received free passes for his friends to watch the filming, he immediately asked Andrew and Gino to come along.

Andrew and Gino were allowed half a day off school. They left at lunchtime and caught the bus to the set. A security guard was blocking the gate. He looked the boys up and down, then raised his eyebrows. Gino pushed Andrew forward.

"No entry for autographs," the man shouted. "You'll have to wait until they finish." He looked at his watch and then at them. "So if I were you, I'd get back to school before the teachers notice that you're gone." The security guard adjusted his black t-shirt and turned to leave.

"You don't understand," Andrew said. "We know one of the actors. He invited us to come and watch them film."

"Yeah sure, kid. If I had a buck for every time I heard that, I'd be rich."

"Show him the passes," Gino whispered.

Andrew fumbled in his pocket. "Wait," he said. "Look — we have passes."

The guard turned around. He examined the passes, then smiled. "Why didn't you say so in the first place?" He pushed a button and the heavy gate slid open. "So, who do you know? Hang on, don't tell me ... You look a bit like Kylie Minnow. I bet you're her kid brother."

Andrew blushed. "Not quite. I'm Billy Rose's brother."

The guard frowned. "Billy Rose?" Then he grinned. "Billy! You mean the new kid? The one with the great smile?"

Andrew hesitated. He'd expected him to say, Billy, the one with Down's Syndrome. That's how people usually described his brother. Andrew pictured Billy's face. He remembered the way Billy smiled when they went fishing. The guard was right — Billy did have a great smile. It lit up his whole face. "Yep, that's the one," he mumbled, realizing that he hadn't shared many of Billy's smiles lately.

"Which way do we go?" Gino asked the guard.

"See those trucks over there by the trees?" Gino nodded. "Well, they should be filming on the other side of it. Down by the creek."

"Let's go." Gino grabbed Andrew's arm and dragged him toward the trucks.

Billy was sitting amidst a group of actors. As they walked closer, Andrew heard them talking and laughing together.

"Hey, look!" Gino gasped. "That's Kylie Minnow. Wow! She looks even better in real life."

Andrew didn't answer. He was watching Billy whisper something to Kylie. Andrew stared. His brother, Billy, was chatting to Kylie Minnow and she was hanging off every word!

Andrew thought about how he'd been treating Billy lately. He remembered how he'd said Billy would embarrass them at the school play. Then he remembered how he'd ignored Billy at the mall. He remembered pretending not to notice his new friends making fun of him.

Then he remembered the look of hurt that crossed Billy's face when he'd realized that his big brother wasn't so special after all.

"Hey, what's wrong?" Gino asked. "C'mon, let's go and get their autographs."

Andrew shrugged. He couldn't. He was too embarrassed to tell Gino that, while he'd been showing off with his new friends, his brother had quietly gone on with his own life. Andrew hung his head. His brother was indeed the real star here.

Billy turned around and saw Andrew and Gino. A huge grin appeared on his face. "Andrew!" he yelled. Kylie looked up as Billy knocked over a chair hurrying to greet his older brother.

"I told Kylie you'd be here soon," Billy said, tugging Andrew's arm. "Come and meet everyone."

"In a moment, Billy. First ... I want to say, umm ... I want to say that ..."

"Ten minutes until your scene, Billy," a girl called.

Billy studied Andrew's eyes, then smiled. "It's okay," he said. "I think I understand."

Billy grabbed Andrew's hand, then remembering his brother's words at the supermarket, he let go. Andrew blushed. "I'm sorry, Billy, but we really are a bit too old to hold hands," he said. "But hey, I think it's okay for us to do this." He let his arm rest loosely over Billy's shoulders.

Billy beamed. "Okay!" he said. "Now, come on. I want you to meet my new friends!"

- INSTALL ELECTRICAL BREAKERS FOR ENTIRE SHOP WITHIN EASY REACH, CIRCUIT-RATED FOR SUFFICIENT AMPERAGE

- STOCK FIRST AID KIT WITH MATERIALS TO TREAT CUTS, GASHES, SPLINTERS, FOREIGN OBJECTS AND CHEMICALS IN EYES, AND BURNS

- HAVE TELEPHONE IN SHOP TO CALL FOR HELP

- INSTALL FIRE EXTINGUISHER RATED FOR A-, B-, AND C-CLASS FIRES

- WEAR EYE PROTECTION AT ALL TIMES

- LOCK CABINETS AND POWER TOOLS TO PROTECT CHILDREN AND INEXPERIENCED VISITORS

- USE DUST COLLECTOR TO KEEP SHOP DUST AT A MINIMUM

- WEAR SHIRT SLEEVES ABOVE ELBOWS

- WEAR CLOSE-FITTING CLOTHES

- WEAR LONG PANTS

- REMOVE WATCHES, RINGS, OR JEWELRY

- KEEP TABLE AND FENCE SURFACES WAXED AND RUST-FREE

- WEAR THICK-SOLED SHOES, PREFERABLY WITH STEEL TOES

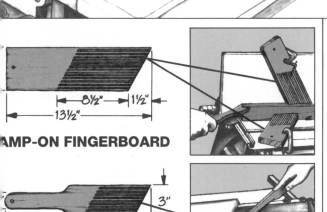

8½" 1½"
13½"

AMP-ON FINGERBOARD

3"

6" 2" 5" 1½"
14½"

D-HELD FINGERBOARD

PROTECTION

WEAR FULL FACE SHIELD DURING LATHE TURNING, ROUTING, AND OTHER OPERATIONS THAT MAY THROW CHIPS

WEAR DUST MASK DURING SANDING AND SAWING

WEAR VAPOR MASK DURING FINISHING

WEAR EAR PROTECTORS DURING ROUTING, PLANING, AND LONG, CONTINUOUS POWER TOOL OPERATION

WEAR SAFETY GLASSES OR GOGGLES AT ALL TIMES

WEAR RUBBER GLOVES FOR HANDLING DANGEROUS CHEMICALS

THE WORKSHOP COMPANION®

ADVANCED ROUTING

TECHNIQUES FOR BETTER WOODWORKING

by Nick Engler

Rodale Press
Emmaus, Pennsylvania

If you have any questions or comments concerning this book, please write:
Rodale Press
Book Readers' Service
33 East Minor Street
Emmaus, PA 18098

About the Author: Nick Engler is an experienced wood-worker, writer, and teacher. He worked as a luthier for many years, making traditional American musical instruments before he founded *Hands On!* magazine. Today, he contributes to several woodworking magazines and teaches woodworking at the University of Cincinnati. He has written more than 30 books.

Series Editor: Jeff Day
Editors: Bob Moran
            Roger Yepsen
Copy Editor: Barbara Webb
Graphic Designer: Linda Watts
Graphic Artists: Mary Jane Favorite
                    Chris Walendzak
Master Craftsman: Jim McCann
Photographer: Karen Callahan
Cover Photographer: Mitch Mandel
Proofreader: Hue Park
Indexer: Beverly Bremer
Typesetting by Computer Typography, Huber Heights, Ohio
Interior and endpaper illustrations by Mary Jane Favorite
Produced by Bookworks, Inc., West Milton, Ohio

The author and editors who compiled this book have tried to make all the contents as accurate and as correct as possible. Plans, illustrations, photographs, and text have all been carefully checked and cross-checked. However, due to the variability of local conditions, construction materials, personal skill, and so on, neither the author nor Rodale Press assumes any responsibility for any injuries suffered, or for damages or other losses incurred that result from the material presented herein. All instructions and plans should be carefully studied and clearly understood before beginning construction.

Special Thanks to:

University of Cincinnati
Cincinnati, Ohio

Victoria Hathaway
West Milton, Ohio

Wertz Hardware
West Milton, Ohio

Winterthur Museum
Winterthur, Delaware

Library of Congress Cataloging-in-Publication Data

Engler, Nick.
    Advanced routing/by Nick Engler.
        p.   cm. — (The workshop companion)
    Includes index.
    ISBN 0–87596–578–4   hardcover
    1. Routers (Tools).   2. Woodwork.   I. Title   II. Series:
Engler, Nick.   Workshop companion.
TT203.5.E53   1993
684'.083—dc20   92–37950
                                                    CIP

                10   9   hardcover

CONTENTS

TECHNIQUES

PROJECTS

TECHNIQUES

1

ROUTER JOINERY

Almost any woodworking joint that you can imagine can be made with a router. This includes not only simple joints such as dadoes and rabbets, but also most complex joinery, including coped joints, mortise-and-tenon joints, dovetail joints, and finger joints. Furthermore, *there is more than one way to rout each joint!* In many cases, there are several router techniques and routing setups that you might use to achieve the same result.

For instance, you might rout a tongue-and-groove joint using ordinary straight bits. Cut a groove down the center of one edge, then cut two rabbets in the adjoining edge to make a tenon. Or, you might save setup time by using a set of matched cutters, one to cut a groove and the other to form a tenon. You could perform both of these operations with either a hand-held or a table-mounted router. That makes four different methods for cutting

the same joint, and we haven't exhausted all the possibilities yet.

There are, in fact, so many joints that you can make on a router and so many ways to rout them, that you couldn't fit them in a single book, let alone a chapter. So instead of trying to cover as many joints as possible, I'm going to present just a few popular complex joints, show several different ways to make each of them, and discuss the various advantages of each method.

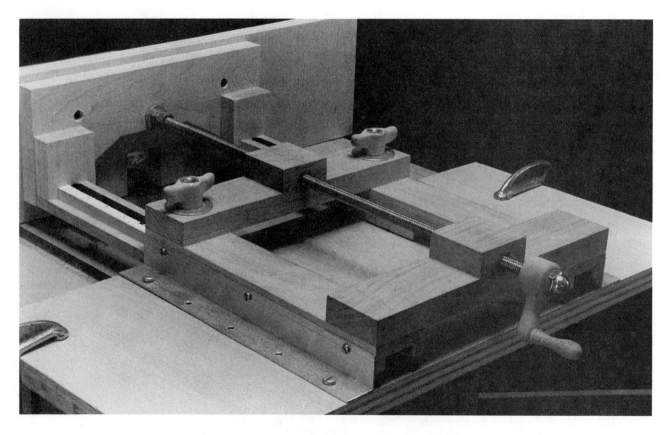

ROUTING MORTISES AND TENONS

Mortise-and-tenon joints are one of the best ways to join the members of a wooden frame, and routing is one of the quickest and most accurate ways that you can make them.

There are three common ways to rout a mortise, using ordinary routing accessories and jigs:

■ Rout the mortise with a hand-held router, using a straight bit to cut the wood and an edge guide to guide the router. (*See Figure 1-1.*) This is perhaps the simplest and most straightforward method. The only setup that you must do is adjust the depth of cut and the edge guide. The major drawback is that the edge of a board may not safely support the base of the router.

■ Rout the mortise with a table-mounted router, using a straight bit to cut the workpiece and a fence to guide it. (*See Figure 1-2.*) This is a much safer method for cutting mortises in the narrow edges of boards. It does, however, require more setup time.

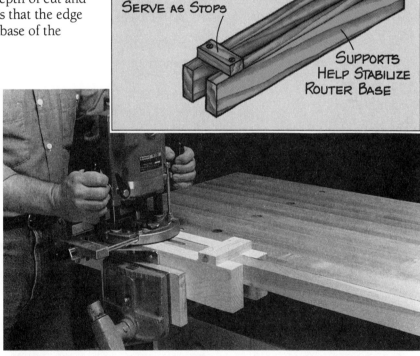

STRETCHERS HOLD THE SUPPORTS FLUSH WITH THE TOP EDGE OF THE WORKPIECE AND ALSO SERVE AS STOPS

SUPPORTS HELP STABILIZE ROUTER BASE

1-1 When routing mortises with a hand-held router, you may wish to clamp auxiliary boards to the faces of the workpiece to provide extra support for the router base. To quickly position these boards, fasten them together with two stretchers, as shown. The stretchers can also serve as stops to help you begin and end the mortise cut. **Note:** It's much easier to rout mortises with plunge routers; you simply lower the bit into the wood. If you use a standard router, you must adjust the depth-of-cut, then rock or swing the bit into the cut.

1-2 A table-mounted router and a fence offer more support when cutting mortises, but you cannot see the cut as you make it. To compensate for this, you must lay out the beginning and end of the mortise on a visible surface of the workpiece. Place a piece of masking tape on the router table in front of the bit and mark the cutting diameter of the bit on it. Feeding the wood from right to left (so the rotation of the bit helps hold it against the fence), start cutting the mortise with the left layout line on the workpiece lined up with the left mark on the router table. Stop cutting when the two right-hand marks align.

Not only do you have to position the fence and measure the depth of cut, you also have to lay out the beginning and end of the mortise on the outside of the workpiece (where it's visible) and mark the cutting diameter of the bit on the router table. This tells you where to start and stop cutting.

■ Fasten a template to the workpiece and mount a guide collar on the base of a hand-held router. Following the inside edge of the template with the guide collar, rout the mortise with a straight bit. (SEE FIGURE 1-3.) The *first* mortise you make with this setup takes a good deal of time because you must make the template. After the first mortise, however, the cutting goes very quickly. Furthermore, you're assured that all the mortises you cut are exactly the same.

FOR BEST RESULTS

When routing deep mortises, remember to make the cut in several passes, routing no more than 1/4 inch deep with each pass. If the wood is very hard or tends to chip and splinter, rout the mortise in 1/8- or even 1/16-inch-deep passes. Also, use a spiral straight bit to help clear the chips from the mortise as you cut — this is especially important when you're using a hand-held router and the bit is positioned over the work. The chips tend to fall down into the mortise and clog it.

To create a tenon to fit a mortise, you must cut one or more rabbets in the end of the adjoining workpiece. Each rabbet will create a shoulder of the tenon.

There are two common ways to rout tenons, using simple routing equipment:

■ Rout the tenons with a hand-held router and straight bit, using a straightedge to guide the router. (SEE FIGURES 1-4 AND 1-5.) This is a simple operation, but you can only cut one side of the tenon at a time. An ordinary tenon with shoulders at the top, bottom, and sides requires four separate cuts — and four setups. To do this with reasonable speed, you must create a jig to position the straightedge on the workpiece.

■ Rout the tenons with a table-mounted router and straight bit, using the fence as a stop and a miter gauge to feed the workpiece past the bit. (SEE FIGURE 1-6.) Again, you can only cut one side of the tenon at a time, but the miter gauge and fence position the wood for each cut. There is no need to build a jig or setup for each cut.

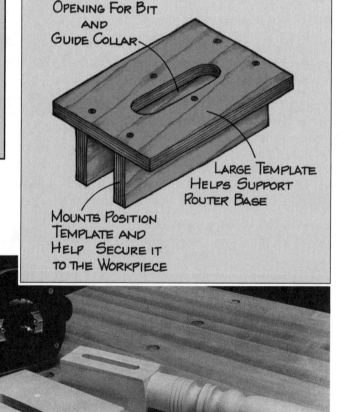

OPENING FOR BIT AND GUIDE COLLAR

LARGE TEMPLATE HELPS SUPPORT ROUTER BASE

MOUNTS POSITION TEMPLATE AND HELP SECURE IT TO THE WORKPIECE

1-3 A mortising template need be nothing more than a hole cut in a piece of plywood or particleboard. The size and shape of the hole depend on the size and shape of the mortise you wish to cut, the diameter of the guide collar, and the diameter of the routing bit. When you make the template, cut it large enough that it will support the base of the router. You may also wish to fasten the template to one or more mounting boards. These mounting boards position the template and provide an easy way to clamp it to the workpiece.

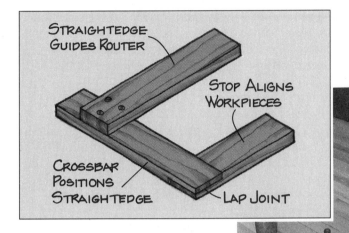

STRAIGHTEDGE
GUIDES ROUTER

STOP ALIGNS
WORKPIECES

CROSSBAR
POSITIONS
STRAIGHTEDGE

LAP JOINT

1-4 The simple jig shown makes it easy to rout tenons with a hand-held router. Place the jig over the workpiece, butting the crossbar against the face or edge, and the stop against the end. Clamp the jig in place and rout one side of the tenon, guiding the router along the straight-edge. To save time, you may wish to rout several workpieces at once.

1-5 You can use this same jig to rout all four sides of a tenon. Lay each workpiece face up to rout the cheeks, and edge up (as shown) to rout the top and bottom surfaces. If you're cutting several workpieces at one time, stack them edge to edge or face to face. Clamp them together to prevent them from shifting as you cut.

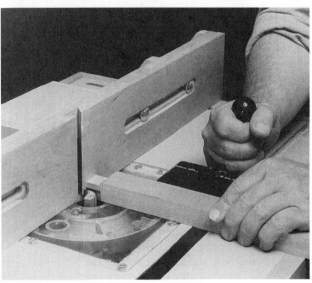

1-6 If you rout tenons with a table-mounted router, use the miter gauge to feed the work and the fence to position the stock. Make sure that the fence is parallel to the miter gauge slot. Otherwise, the tenon shoulders may not be square to the edge of the board. As you work, feed the work from right to left (as you face the fence) so the rotation of the bit holds the stock against the fence.

All the mortising techniques described so far create mortises with *round* corners and tenons with *square* corners. To fit the two together, you must either square the corners of the mortises with a chisel or round the corners of the tenons with a rasp. There is, however, a method you can use to cut a tenon with round corners and save some work. Make a template much like the mortising template, attach it to the *end* of a workpiece, and cut the tenon with a hand-held router, straight bit, and guide collar. (*SEE FIGURE 1-7.*) An additional advantage to this setup is that you can cut all four sides of the tenon in one operation.

Each of the procedures outlined so far requires at least two setups to make one mortise-and-tenon joint — one to make the mortise and another for the tenon. Also, the sizes of the mortises and tenons you can make with each jig or setup are limited. For example, if you use the router table to cut mortises, you must adjust the setup every time you change the size of the mortise or the workpiece. Likewise, a tenoning template will cut only one size tenon and will only fit over a workpiece of a certain thickness.

You can, however, purchase or build jigs that cut *both* mortises and tenons. All of these jigs offer interchangeable templates to cut mortises and tenons of different sizes. Usually, the templates are paired so you can cut a mortise and the tenon that fits it without changing the entire setup. (*SEE FIGURES 1-8 THROUGH 1-10.*) These jigs may not be worth the money it takes to buy them or the effort required to build them if you only cut mortises and tenons occasionally, or if you always make the same size mortises and tenons. In these cases, one of the simpler setups or jigs may serve you better. However, if you must make a lot of mortises and tenons in a variety of sizes, then a mortise-and-tenon jig is a good investment.

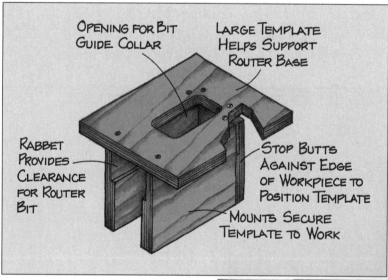

1-7 The tenoning template jig works in much the same way as the mortising template jig, with several important changes. When assembling the jig, attach a stop to the mounts, as shown — this will position the template over the workpiece. Also, rabbet the inside faces of the mount and stop to provide clearance for the router bit. When mounting the template, secure it so the opening is over the *end* of the workpiece rather than the edge. Make sure the end of the board is flush with the bottom surface of the template.

TRY THIS TRICK

In addition to cutting mortise-and-tenon joints, you can also use these techniques and fixtures to make mortise-and-spline joints. Instead of cutting a mortise and a tenon to fit, rout two matching mortises. Cut a single spline to fit both mortises, straddling the joint between them. As long as you get a good fit, this joint will be just as strong as a traditional mortise and tenon. Mortise-and-spline joints are often used to reinforce miter joints and other assemblies where the grain direction of the adjoining boards won't allow you to make a strong tenon.

1-8 Many commercial jigs that will cut mortises and tenons mount the router sideways so the bit is held horizontally. On this particular jig, the router moves up and down, while the workpiece — which is clamped to a movable table — moves side to side and front to back. As shown in the inset, a "follower" traces the contour of the template while the router cuts a duplicate of the shape in the workpiece. In addition to templates for various sizes of mortises and tenons, manufacturers usually offer templates for finger joints and dovetail joints.

1-9 This shopmade mortise-and- tenon jig fits in a woodworking vise, and holds workpieces while you cut mortises and tenons with a hand-held router and straight bit. The router is guided by a guide collar and interchangeable templates. To cut a mortise in the face or edge of a workpiece, secure the wood in the jig *horizontally.* Follow the inside edge of the template with the collar as you cut.

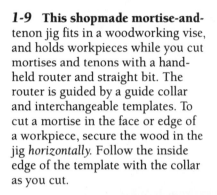

1-10 When cutting a tenon in the end of a workpiece, mount the work-piece vertically. Use the same basic technique to rout the tenon as you used for the mortises, following the inside edge of the template with the guide collar. However, when making the tenon, you must be careful to keep the collar firmly against the template at all times. (See the plans for the "Mortise-and-Tenon Jig," along with instructions on how to make the templates, beginning on the facing page.)

MORTISE-AND-TENON JIG

This mortise-and-tenon jig allows you to cut both mortises and tenons with a hand-held router, guide collar, and straight bit. The jig holds the work either horizontally or vertically between the faces, and positions a template above the work. The template is interchangeable, allowing you to cut many different sizes of mortises and tenons.

The openings in the template determine the length and width of the mortise or the thickness and width of the tenon. (The depth of the mortise and the length of the tenon are controlled by the router's depth of cut.) The size of the openings depends on the dimensions of the mortise or tenon you want to cut, the diameter of the router bit, and the diameter of the guide collar.

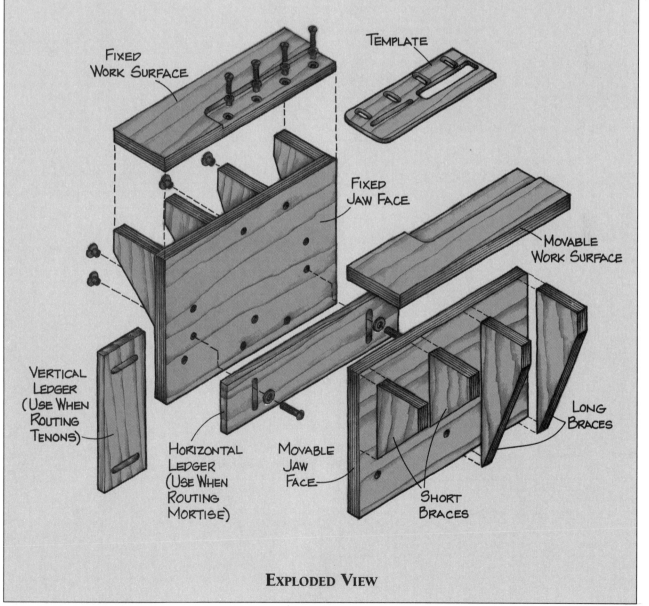

FIXED
WORK SURFACE

TEMPLATE

FIXED
JAW FACE

MOVABLE
WORK SURFACE

VERTICAL
LEDGER
(USE WHEN
ROUTING
TENONS)

HORIZONTAL
LEDGER
(USE WHEN
ROUTING
MORTISE)

MOVABLE
JAW
FACE

SHORT
BRACES

LONG
BRACES

EXPLODED VIEW

(continued) ▷

MORTISE-AND-TENON JIG — CONTINUED

To figure the size of a template opening for routing a particular mortise, subtract the diameter of the router bit from the outside diameter of the guide collar to find the difference between the two. Add this *difference* to both the length and width of the mortise to get the length and width of the opening. For example, if you wish to cut a $\frac{1}{2}$-inch-wide, 2-inch-long mortise with a $\frac{3}{8}$-inch-diameter straight bit and a $\frac{5}{8}$-inch-diameter collar, the template opening must be $\frac{3}{4}$ inch wide and $2\frac{1}{4}$ inch long:

$$(\tfrac{5}{8} - \tfrac{3}{8}) + \tfrac{1}{2} = \tfrac{3}{4},$$
$$\text{and } (\tfrac{5}{8} - \tfrac{3}{8}) + 2 = 2\tfrac{1}{4}.$$

To figure the size of a template opening for routing a tenon, again find the difference between the diameter of the outside guide collar and the diameter of the straight bit. Add *twice* the diameter of the guide collar to the thickness and width of the tenon, then subtract the difference. To cut a $\frac{1}{2}$-inch-thick, 2-inch-wide tenon to fit the mortise in the previous example, you need a template opening $1\frac{3}{8}$ inches wide and 3 inches long:

$$(2 \times \tfrac{5}{8}) + \tfrac{1}{2} - (\tfrac{5}{8} - \tfrac{3}{8}) = 1\tfrac{1}{2},$$
$$\text{and } (2 \times \tfrac{5}{8}) + 2 - (\tfrac{5}{8} - \tfrac{3}{8}) = 3.$$

If you're making small or medium-sized mortise-and-tenon joints, the templates for this jig are large enough to cut two openings side by side — one for the mortise and the other for the matching tenon. Only when you need to cut large mortises and tenons do you have to make separate templates.

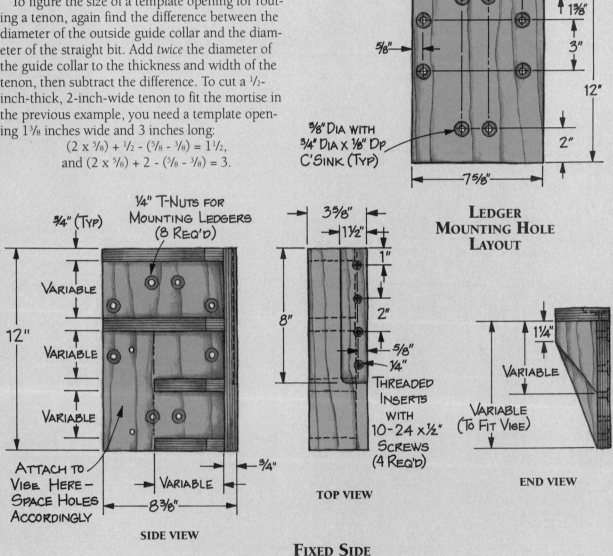

LEDGER MOUNTING HOLE LAYOUT

SIDE VIEW

TOP VIEW

END VIEW

FIXED SIDE

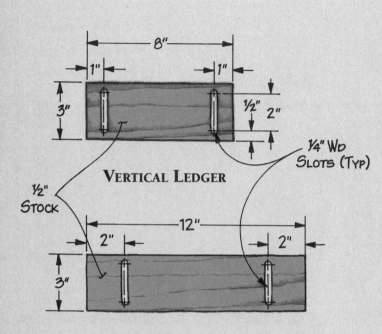

VERTICAL LEDGER

8"

1" 1"

3"

½" 2"

¼" WD SLOTS (TYP)

½" STOCK

12"

2" 2"

3"

HORIZONTAL LEDGER

NOTE: Mount ledgers with ¼"-20 x 1¼" RH machine screws (2 Req'd).

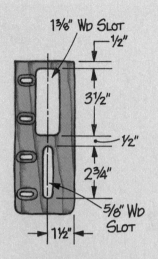

SAMPLE TEMPLATE

1⅜" WD SLOT

½"

3½"

½"

2¾"

5/8" WD SLOT

1½"

(FOR ⅜" X 2½" MORTISE & TENON, USING ⅜" STRAIGHT BIT & 5/8" GUIDE COLLAR)

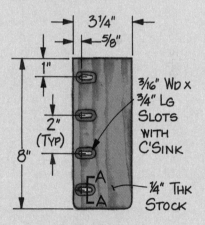

BLANK TEMPLATE

3¼"

5/8"

1"

2" (TYP)

8"

3/16" WD X ¾" LG SLOTS WITH C'SINK

A A

¼" THK STOCK

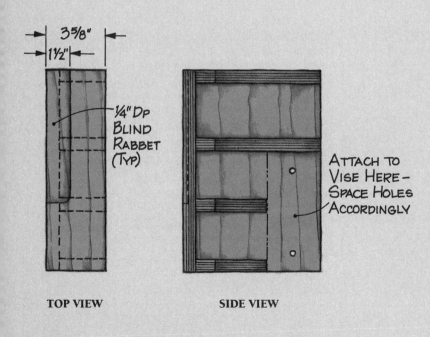

3⅝"

1½"

¼" DP BLIND RABBET (TYP)

ATTACH TO VISE HERE – SPACE HOLES ACCORDINGLY

TOP VIEW   **SIDE VIEW**

MOVABLE SIDE

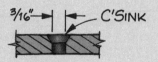

3/16"   C'SINK

SECTION A

COUNTERSINK DETAIL

(continued) ▷

Mortise-and-Tenon Jig — continued

1 **To set up the jig, first** remove the wooden faces from an ordinary woodworking vise, then attach the faces of the jig to the metal jaws. As shown in the working drawings, this jig is designed to mount in a 7-inch-wide Record (52D) vise. However, you can easily adjust the dimensions to mount it in any woodworking vise. You can also adapt the design to fasten to the wooden jaws of a traditional all-wood vise.

2 **Attach a ledger to the front** face of the jig, positioning it to hold the workpiece. Use the horizontal ledger for routing mortises, or the vertical ledger for routing tenons. Clamp a test piece in the jig by closing the jaws of the vise. The top surface of the test piece should be flush with the bottom of the rabbet that holds the template.

3 **Secure the template to the** fixed work surface of the jig, centering it over the test piece. If you cannot center the template, you may have to readjust the position of the ledger. When the ledger and template are properly adjusted, cut a mortise or a tenon in the test piece. Carefully measure the results and, if necessary, readjust the components. When you're sure the setup is correct, cut good wood.

ROUTING INTERLOCKING JOINTS

To rout interlocking assemblies such as finger joints and dovetail joints, you must be able to position each cut very accurately. If just one finger or dovetail is miscut, the entire joint may be ruined. There are several methods for precise positioning, all of which rely on fixtures or templates.

MAKING FINGER JOINTS

To rout a finger joint, you must cut multiple tenons (fingers) in the adjoining ends of the boards you wish to assemble. The fingers on one board must fit the notches between the fingers on the other. Normally, these fingers are evenly spaced — the fingers and notches are all the same width.

To rout an evenly spaced finger joint, use a table-mounted router and a simple finger jig. Cut the joint with a straight bit, making the fingers and the notches as wide as the diameter of the bit. (*SEE FIGURES 1-11 THROUGH 1-13.*)

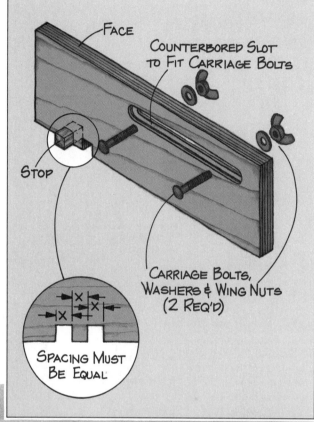

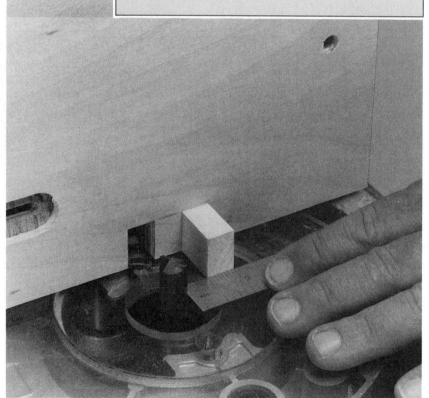

1-11 To rout finger joints with evenly spaced fingers, make a wooden fence for the miter gauge on your router table. This fence should be adjustable, so you can slide it left or right. Using a straight bit, cut a notch in the bottom edge. Cut a stop to fit this notch and glue it in place, as shown. Slide the miter gauge fence to the right so the distance between the stop and the bit is exactly the same as the diameter of the bit, and cut another notch. **Note:** You should cut several test pieces to make sure this setup is adjusted properly before cutting good stock.

1-12 To rout the first board in a finger joint, adjust the depth of cut so the straight bit is about $^{1}/_{32}$ inch higher than the board is thick. Place the board against the finger jig, end down, with one edge against the stop. To prevent tear-out, sandwich the good stock between scraps. Clamp the board and the scraps to the face of the jig. Turn on the router and feed the board into the bit, cutting the first notch. Loosen the clamp, move the board so the notch is over the stop, and tighten the clamp again. Cut a second notch. Repeat until you have cut fingers and notches all across the end of the first board.

1-13 You must use the first board as a spacer to position the second board for its initial cut. Turn the first board around, face for face, and hook the first notch you cut over the stop. There should be just one finger between the stop and the notch. Place the second board in the jig and butt the edge against the first. Clamp the second board in place and remove the first. Make the first cut in the second board, then continue cutting in exactly the same way you cut the first board. When you've finished cutting all the fingers and notches, the ends of the two boards should interlock.

To rout a finger joint with unevenly spaced fingers and notches, you must use a *positioning jig* to align the adjoining boards for each cut. A positioning jig moves a fence, guide, or cutting tool a precise distance. This enables you to make equally precise cuts, although it takes a good deal of planning to figure out how far to move the jig for each cut. You can choose from several commercial positioning jigs (*See Figure 1-14*), or you can make your own. For plans for a shopmade "Positioning Jig," see page 19.

To rout an unevenly spaced finger joint with a positioning jig, you'll also need a fence to attach to the jig and a "pusher" — a fixture that will hold the boards square to the fence as you push them along it. Mount the positioning jig and fence to your router table and "zero" the fence to the bit. (*See Figure 1-15.*) Plan how far to move the jig for each cut in each board. This will depend on not only the joint you want to cut, but the diameter of the router bit you use to cut it. (*See Figure 1-16.*) Then make the cuts in both boards, forming the interlocking fingers and notches. Use the positioning jig to move the fence the necessary distance before each cut. (*See Figures 1-17 and 1-18.*)

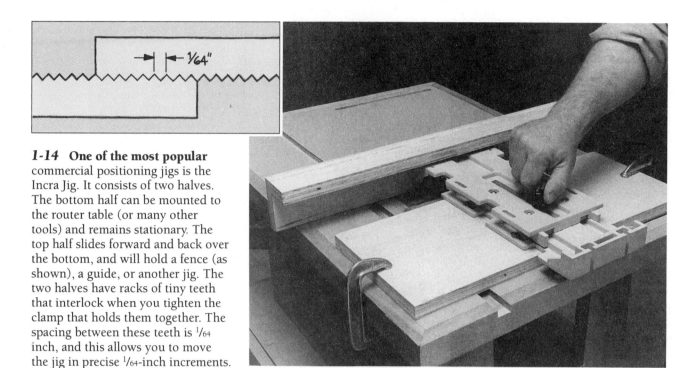

1-14 One of the most popular
commercial positioning jigs is the
Incra Jig. It consists of two halves.
The bottom half can be mounted to
the router table (or many other
tools) and remains stationary. The
top half slides forward and back over
the bottom, and will hold a fence (as
shown), a guide, or another jig. The
two halves have racks of tiny teeth
that interlock when you tighten the
clamp that holds them together. The
spacing between these teeth is $1/64$
inch, and this allows you to move
the jig in precise $1/64$-inch increments.

1-15 To use a positioning jig to
align the stock for each cut, you
must work from a reference or "0"
point. To zero the fence, first extend
the jig as far forward as it will go. If
you're using the shopmade jig shown
on page 19, extend it until the scale
reads "0." Place the jig on the router
table so the bit is centered in the
cutout in the fence and the front
edge of the bit is flush with the face
of the fence. (The bit should be
covered by the cutout.) Clamp the
mounting board to the router table
and use a straightedge, as shown, to
check the relative position of the bit
and fence. If it has shifted from the
zero position, loosen one of the
clamps and tap the positioning jig
backward or forward until the fence
is zeroed. Tighten the clamp again.

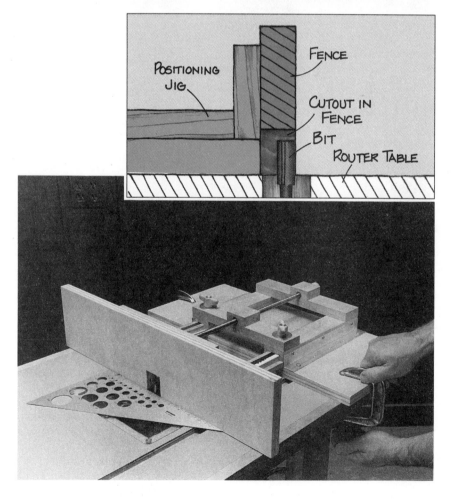

1-16 Draw the finger joint to scale exactly as you want to cut it. If the joint is very small, you may want to draw it two or four times larger than full-scale. Carefully measure the positions of the fingers and notches as you draw. Designate one edge of the joint as the "zero" edge — this is the edge that will rest against the fence as you cut. Then plan how far you must move the fence before making each cut. (On the positioning jig that will be used to make this joint, one turn of the handle moves the fence 1/16 inch, and the amount of movement has been translated into the number of turns required to make that movement.) *Remember to allow for the diameter of the straight bit!* For example, when the fence is moved 1 inch from the zero position, a 3/8-inch-diameter bit

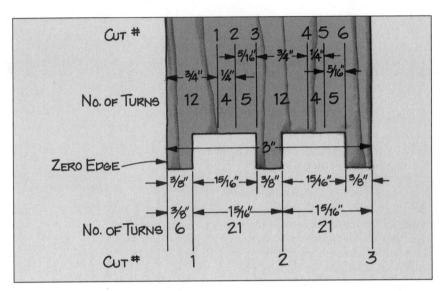

will cut a 3/8-inch-wide notch with the *farthest* cheek 1 inch from the zero edge of the board. The other

cheek will be 5/8 inch from the edge. The cuts shown here were planned for a 3/8-inch-diameter straight bit.

1-17 Before the first cut, adjust the depth of cut so the straight bit is about 1/32 inch higher than the thickness of the stock you wish to join. Use the positioning jig to move the fence the necessary distance prior to each cut. If you're using the shop-made positioning jig shown, loosen the clamping nuts and turn the handle, counting the revolutions — one full turn moves the fence precisely 1/16 inch. Double-check the position on the scale, then secure the clamping nuts.

1-18 To make each cut, feed the board into the bit with the pusher, keeping the end of the board against the router table and the zero edge against the fence. The face of the board should be square to the fence. To prevent tear-out, sandwich the board between scraps. Clamp the good stock and the scraps to the pusher to prevent them from shifting. **Note:** If you're making several identical pieces, you can stack them face to face and rout them all at once.

MAKING DOVETAIL JOINTS

When routing dovetails, the principle is the same as it is for routing finger joints — the tails on one board must fit the notches between the pins on the other. However, because the tails and pins are sloped, a good deal more calculation is required for spacing the cuts. (*See Figure 1-19.*) Furthermore, because the pins and tails are sloped in different directions, the pins cannot be routed in the same manner as the tails. You must either hold the pin and the tail board in different positions as you rout them, or use a different bit and template for each board.

Despite these complications, routing dovetails *is* much faster and easier than doing them by hand. Using a router and a dovetail fixture also takes significantly less time than cutting dovetails on other machines, such as the band saw or table saw. However, making your own dovetail routing jig is time-consuming and requires very accurate machining. You can rout half-blind dovetails with the positioning jig, but this too requires much figuring, and the pro-

cedure is slow and tedious. For all of these reasons, many experienced woodworkers opt to purchase commercial dovetail fixtures rather than make their own.

You can buy fixtures that are designed to cut half-blind dovetails *only,* and those that are designed to cut a variety of dovetail joints, including both half-blind dovetails and through dovetails. The half-blind dovetail jigs are the least expensive and the easiest to operate. Most are configured so that you can cut both the tails and the pins in one step. (*See Figure 1-20.*) Jigs that will cut through dovetails are slightly more complex and a great deal more expensive. Most require that you cut the tails and pins separately, using a dovetail bit to make the tails and a straight bit to make the pins. (*See Figures 1-21 and 1-22.*) All commercial dovetail jigs rely on "comb" templates and guide collars to guide the router. Most of these combs are fixed — you cannot alter the spacing of the pins and tails. However, the Leigh dovetail jig offers an adjustable comb.

1-19 Figuring the spacing of the cuts for a finger joint is fairly straightforward. For example, when routing evenly spaced fingers with a 1/2-inch straight bit, the spacing is twice the diameter of the bit — every 1 inch. Figuring the spacing for dovetail cuts is more complex. Because the dovetails are sloped, there is a triangular area on each pin and tail that overlaps the pins and tails next to it. For this reason, the cuts will be spaced closer together. To rout an evenly spaced dovetail joint with a 1/2-inch-diameter dovetail bit, the cuts are usually spaced 7/8 inch apart. Furthermore, that spacing only works when the slope is 14 degrees and the depth of cut is about 1/2 inch — the overlap changes with the slope and the length of the dovetail.

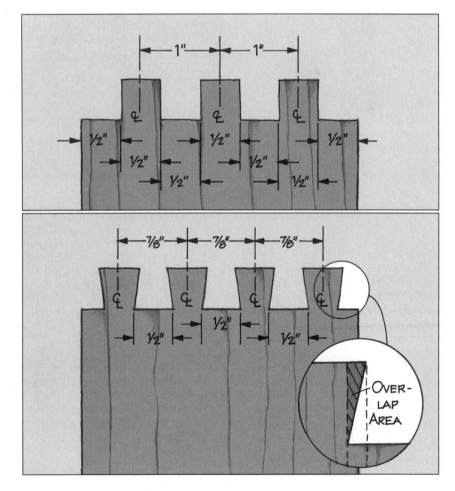

FOR YOUR INFORMATION

Many active craftsmen keep two dovetail fixtures in their shops — one for half-blind dovetails and one for everything else. For instance, I make frequent use of two commercial dovetail routing setups. I have an inexpensive half-blind dovetail jig and an old router that I leave with the necessary guide collar and dovetail bit mounted. Since I rout more half-blind dovetails (mostly for drawer joinery) than any other dovetail joints, this saves much time. On those occasions when I need to rout through dovetails or other special dovetail joints, I use a Leigh jig.

Note: The most difficult part of making your own dovetail template or cutting dovetails with the positioning jig is figuring the overlap of the tails and pins. If you want to tackle the problem, you can draw the joint four to eight times full-scale — this will make it easier to make precise measurements of the overlap. Or, if you want absolute accuracy, you can use a simple trigonometry formula. The overlap (OL) is equal to the tangent of the dovetail slope in degrees (S) times the length of the tails (T):

$$OL = tan\ (S) \times T.$$

1-20 Most half-blind dovetail fixtures allow you to rout the tails and the pins in one step. The tail board is held vertically in the jig, while the pin board is secured horizontally. Using a hand-held router, a dovetail bit, and a guide collar, cut through the tail board and a short distance into the pin board, following the comb with the guide collar. The router will create tails that are rounded on the back side to fit half-round notches between the pins.

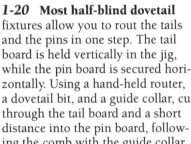

1-21 Most commercial jigs that are designed to cut through dovetails require that you cut them in two steps, using two different templates and router bits. This Leigh jig has a single two-sided comb template — one side for the tails and the other for the pins. The fingers on this comb are movable. You can re-arrange them to change the size of the dovetails or the spacing between them. This lets you space the dove-tails evenly or randomly, whichever you prefer. It also allows you to fit the joint to the project, rather than design the project around the joint.

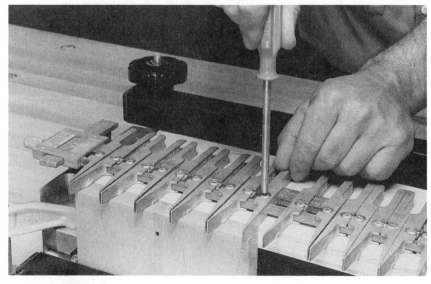

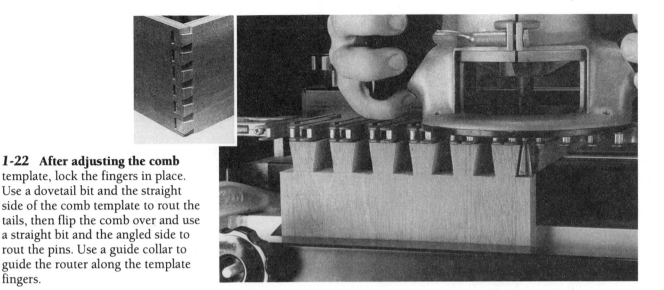

1-22 After adjusting the comb template, lock the fingers in place. Use a dovetail bit and the straight side of the comb template to rout the tails, then flip the comb over and use a straight bit and the angled side to rout the pins. Use a guide collar to guide the router along the template fingers.

POSITIONING JIG

To rout precise joinery with a table-mounted router, you must be able to position the workpiece on the router table accurately. To do this with an ordinary fence is very tedious, requiring careful measuring, test cuts, and readjustment before making each cut. A positioning jig eliminates this tedium. This jig moves a fence or guide a precise distance quickly, with no need for test cuts and readjustment.

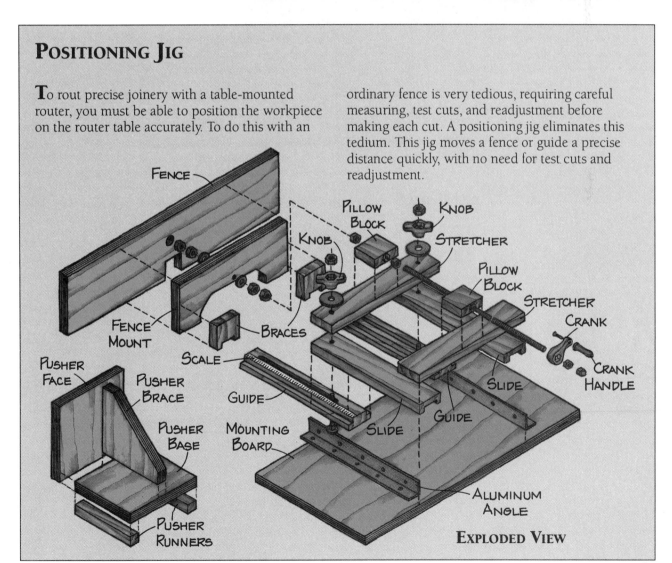

EXPLODED VIEW

(continued) ▷

POSITIONING JIG — CONTINUED

As shown, the jig can be made from scraps of hardwood and common hardware. It uses a standard 3/8-inch-diameter, coarse-threaded rod to move the fence. The thread pitch of this rod is 16 threads per inch. Therefore, one turn of the handle will move the guide precisely 1/16 inch. One half turn will move it 1/32 inch, and one quarter turn, 1/64 inch. By carefully counting the revolutions of the handle, then double-checking the position on the scale, you can move the fence with precision.

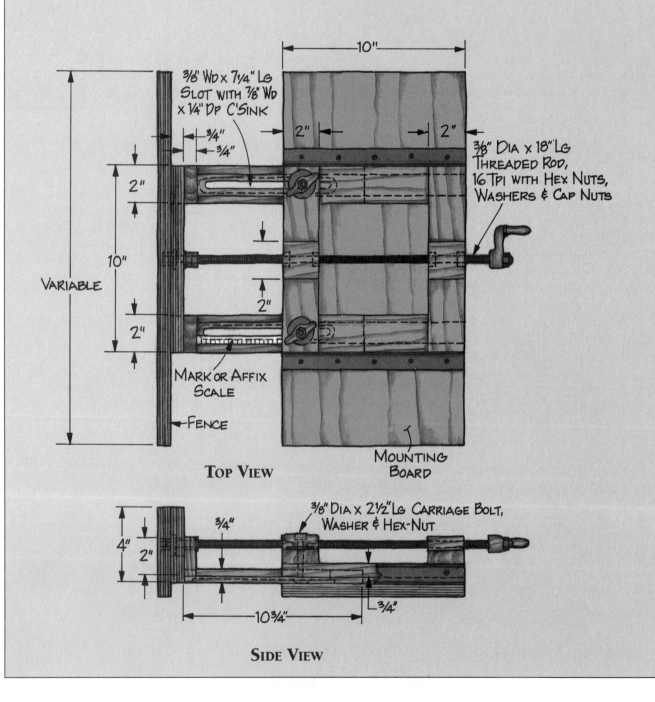

TOP VIEW

SIDE VIEW

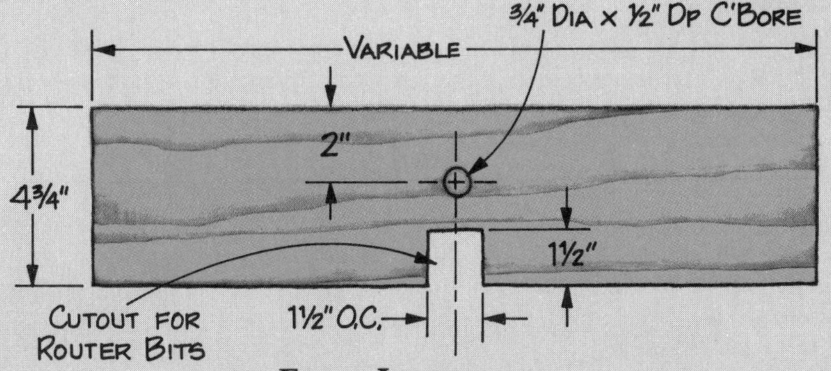
3/4" Dia x 1/2" Dp C'Bore
Variable
2"
4 3/4"
1 1/2"
Cutout for Router Bits
1 1/2" O.C.

Fence Layout

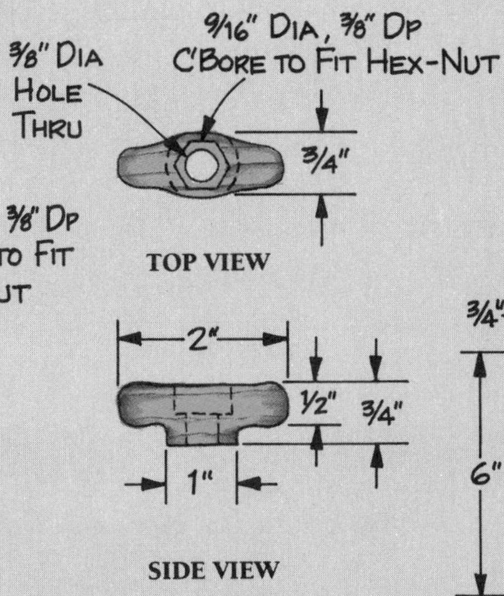
3/8" Dia Hole Thru
9/16" Dia, 3/8" Dp C'Bore to Fit Hex-Nut
3/4"
Top View
2"
1/2"
3/4"
1"
Side View

Knob Detail

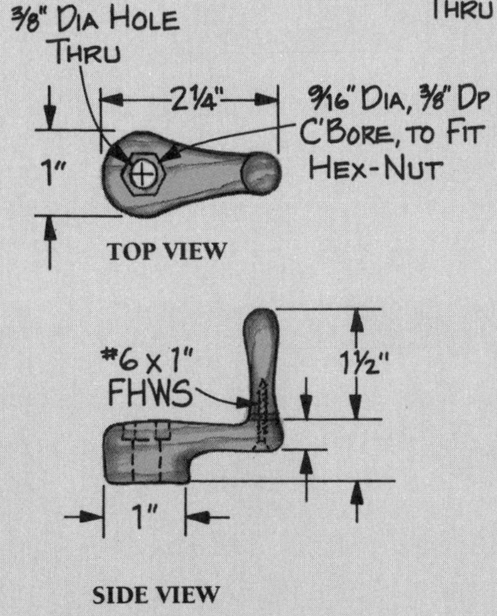
3/8" Dia Hole Thru
2 1/4"
9/16" Dia, 3/8" Dp C'Bore, to Fit Hex-Nut
1"
Top View
#6 x 1" FHWS
1 1/2"
1"
Side View

Crank Detail

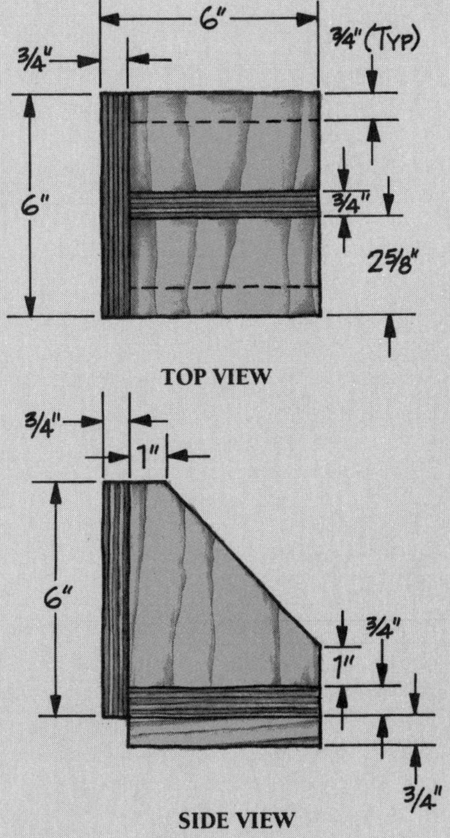
6"
3/4"
3/4" (Typ)
6"
3/4"
2 5/8"
Top View
3/4"
1"
6"
3/4"
1"
3/4"
Side View

Pusher

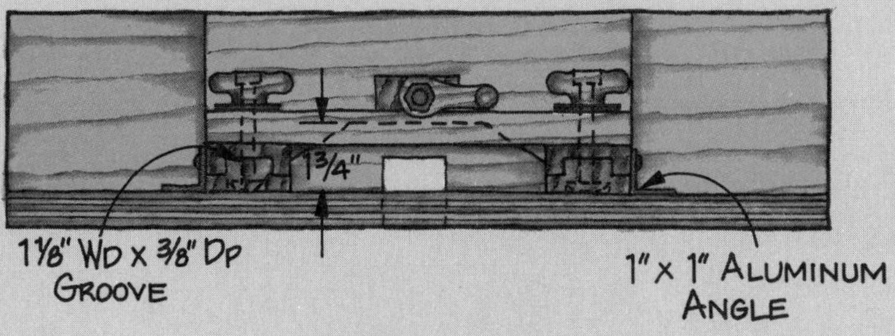
1 3/4"
1 1/8" Wd x 3/8" Dp Groove
1" x 1" Aluminum Angle

End View

(continued) ▷

POSITIONING JIG — CONTINUED

1 **While the construction of** this jig is fairly simple, there are a couple of tricks you should be aware of. First, before setting the nuts that hold the adjusting rod, thread the nuts onto the rod and turn them so they are the proper distance apart. (The outside edge of each nut should be flush with an edge of the pillow block, as shown.) Then mark the surface of each nut that faces up. When you set these nuts in the pillow block, make sure the marked faces are up. And when you thread the adjusting rod through the assembled pillow blocks and nuts, don't worry if the fit seems tight. This is good! If the rod is loose, there may be some slop or "play" in the jig, and this will reduce its precision. In fact, you may need to reset one or more nuts if the rod turns too easily. **Note:** Wax the adjoining surfaces of the guides and slides so the parts operate smoothly.

2 **You must also be careful** that there is no play between the fence mount and the nuts that hold it to the adjusting rod. Carefully tighten the two inside nuts until there is no slop in the joint, but the fit is still loose enough for the adjusting rod to turn. Lock the inside nuts in place by tightening the outside nuts against them.

3   **Don't mount the positioning** jig directly to your router table. Instead, screw it to a mounting board, and clamp this board to your router table. This arrangement lets you zero the jig with router bits of various diameters. (To zero the jig, set the scale to "0" and carefully place it on the router table so the fence face aligns with the cutting edge of the bit.) If the jig were bolted in position on the table, you could only zero it with a single size of bit. Also, the movable mounting board allows you to use the jig with other tools, such as the table saw, band saw, drill press, and lathe.

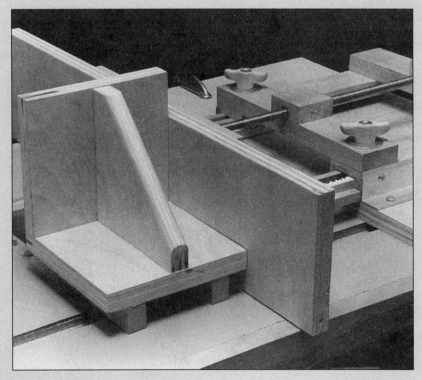

4   **In addition to the positioning** jig and fence, you must also make a "pusher." This simple jig rides along the fence and holds workpieces square to the fence as you rout them.

ROUTING COPED JOINTS

Perhaps the easiest way to make a joint with a router is to cut "coped" joints. In a coped joint, both adjoining surfaces are shaped. Each surface is a mirror image of the other, so the two surfaces mate perfectly. This has two advantages:

■ Often, the shape of the joint *aligns* the adjoining parts so the surfaces are flush or the corners are square.

■ The shape also increases the gluing surfaces and *strengthens* the joint.

There are two types of coped joints, and each must be cut in a different manner. The *reversible* coped joint uses a single router bit, and requires only one setup. However, you must position each of the adjoining members differently as you feed them into the router. This usually requires that you reverse them face for face. (*SEE FIGURES 1-23 AND 1-24.*) The *fitted* coped joint uses two router bits and two different setups. Depending on the joint, the workpieces may or may not be fed differently for each setup. (*SEE FIGURES 1-25 THROUGH 1-27.*)

For a list of common reversible and fitted coped joints that can be cut with router bits, see "Coped Joints" on page 27.

WHERE TO FIND IT

The router bits shown in *FIGURES 1-23 THROUGH 1-27* and in "Coped Joints" on page 27 can be purchased from several mail-order suppliers, including:

Cascade Tools, Inc.
P.O. Box 3110
Bellingham, WA 98227

Woodcraft Supply
210 Wood County Industrial Park
P.O. Box 1686
Parkersburg, WV 26102

1-23 One of the simplest reversible coped joints that you can make on a router is the finger glue joint. This is useful when gluing boards edge to edge or end to end. Rout the fingers in the first workpiece with the top face up, then reverse the second workpiece so the top face is down. Adjust the depth of cut so the top and bottom faces of the adjoining workpieces will be flush when you assemble them. **Note:** The adjoining parts must be of equal thickness.

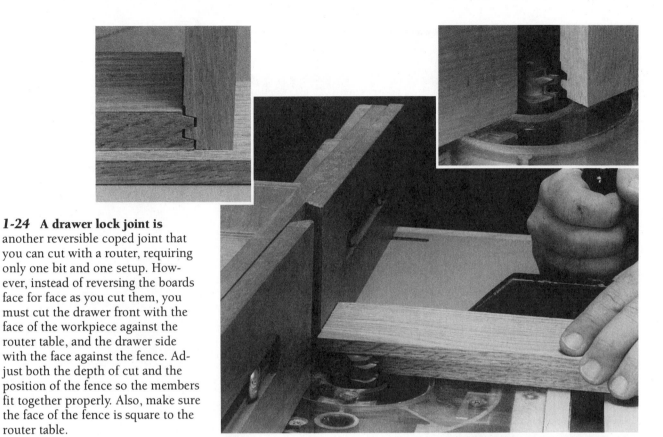

1-24 A drawer lock joint is another reversible coped joint that you can cut with a router, requiring only one bit and one setup. However, instead of reversing the boards face for face as you cut them, you must cut the drawer front with the face of the workpiece against the router table, and the drawer side with the face against the fence. Adjust both the depth of cut and the position of the fence so the members fit together properly. Also, make sure the face of the fence is square to the router table.

1-25 A tongue-and-groove joint is a fitted coped joint, requiring two matched bits. Rout a groove in one edge of each of the workpieces, then change bits and rout a tongue in the other edge. You must carefully adjust the depth of cut for the second cut to match the first, so the faces of the adjoining boards will be flush.

1-26 Stile-and-rail joints also require two matched router bits and are normally used to join the shaped surfaces of frame members. Rout the sticking portion of the joint — the portion with the shape that you want to see — in the *inside* edges of the stiles and rails. Use a fence to guide the stock when routing straight edges, and rely on the pilot bearing only when routing contoured edges.

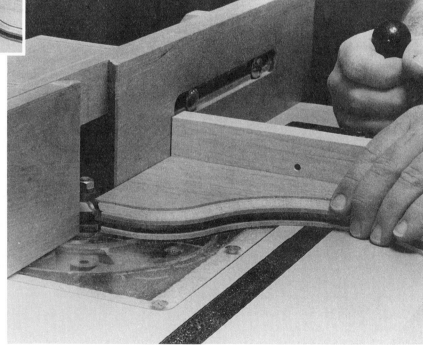

1-27 Rout the coped portion of the stile-and-rail joint in the ends of the rails only. Use a miter gauge to help feed the stock past the bit. To keep the board from chipping out as you finish the cut, back it up with a scrap.

COPED JOINTS

REVERSIBLE JOINTS	FITTED JOINTS

DRAWER LOCK JOINT

To assemble the sides of lipped drawers to the drawer front.

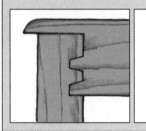 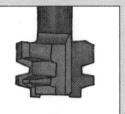

TONGUE-AND-GROOVE JOINT

To assemble boards edge to edge. Used most often in flooring and siding, but can also be used to glue up wide boards.

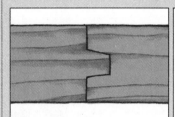 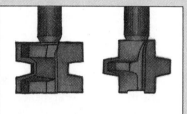

GLUE JOINT

To assemble boards edge to edge.

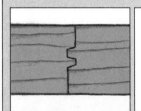 

RULE JOINT

To make folding joints in drop-leaf tables.

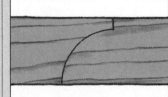 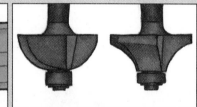

FINGER GLUE JOINT

To join boards edge to edge and end to end. Similar to glue joint, but offers much more gluing surface.

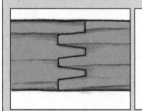 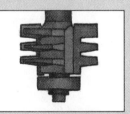

STILE-AND-RAIL JOINT

To join shaped surfaces of frame members that will hold wooden panels. Often used in making cabinet doors.

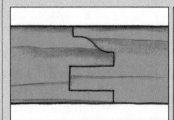 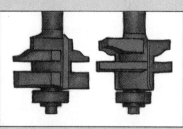

LOCKED MITER JOINT

To make strong 90-degree mitered corners.

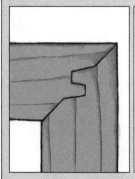 

SASH JOINT

To join the shaped surfaces of "sash work" — frames that will hold glass panels, such as windows and glazed cabinet doors. Similar to stile-and-rail joint, but sticking portion of this joint has rabbet to hold glass rather than groove to hold wooden panel.

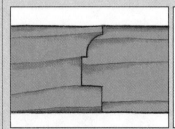 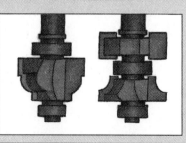

2

PATTERN ROUTING

A router will cut precise patterns in wood — curves, contours, sculpted surfaces, almost any two- or three-dimensional shape. You can rout circles, ovals, or the letters of the alphabet. You can cut exact duplicates of intricately shaped toy parts. You can even make matching cabriole legs or copy a carved molding.

To rout all these shapes and patterns, you must use a template or a jig — or both — to guide the router. Once you've made the necessary fixtures, you can rout a single piece or reproduce the same pattern over and over again. Each routed pattern will be as precise as the template or the jig that you use to make it.

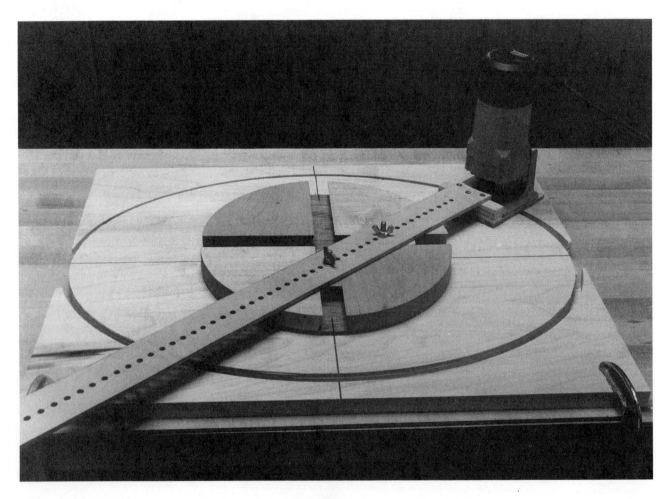

FOLLOWING A TEMPLATE

Perhaps the easiest way to accurately rout a pattern is to guide the router (or the workpiece) with a template. There are three ways to do this:

■ Use a *piloted straight bit* to follow the shape of a template.

■ Follow the edge of the template with a *guide collar.*

■ Or, trace the template with a *pin* that's aligned with a router bit.

PATTERN ROUTING WITH A PILOTED STRAIGHT BIT

There are two types of straight bits that will follow a template and cut a pattern — pattern-cutting bits and flush-trim bits. Both of these have pilot bearings that are exactly the same diameter as the cutting edges. As you rout, the bearing traces the contoured edge of a template while the bit cuts the same contour in the stock. The difference between the two bits is that the bearing on a pattern-cutting bit is mounted on the shank, while that on a flush-trim bit is mounted on the tip. (SEE FIGURE 2-1.)

The position of the bearing determines what patterns can be cut with the bit and how to cut them. Both bits can be used in either a hand-held or a table-mounted router, although a pattern-cutting bit is usually the better choice for a portable router, and a flush-trim bit for a router table. Because the tip of a pattern-cutting bit does the cutting, it will make inside cuts and cutouts with no need to drill starter holes. You can also use it to cut partway through a workpiece, routing contoured grooves or mortises. (SEE FIGURES 2-2 AND 2-3.)

The tip of the flush-trim bit is shielded by the pilot bearing, so it's not as versatile as the pattern-cutting bit. But it does have some advantages. It provides better visibility when used in a table-mounted router — you can watch the template *and* the workpiece as you cut. Also, the bearing helps guard you from the tip of the bit. (SEE FIGURES 2-4 AND 2-5.)

FOR YOUR INFORMATION

Although they can be used for pattern routing, flush-trim bits are designed to trim plastic laminate flush with the underlayment to which it has been applied — hence the name.

FOR BEST RESULTS

Remember that you usually get a smoother cut with less tear-out if you can remove just a little stock at a time. When using pattern-cutting bits, make deep cuts in several passes, cutting just 1/8 to 1/4 inch deeper with each pass. For flush-trim bits, cut the workpiece to a rough shape with a band saw or saber saw so you only have to trim a little waste from the edge with the router.

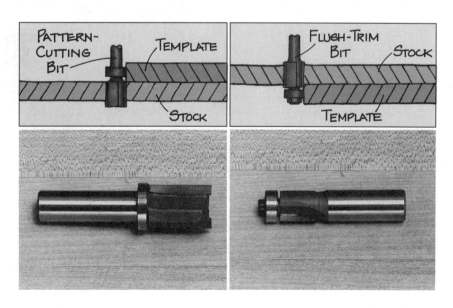

2-1 **You can use both a pattern-** cutting bit (left) and a flush-trim bit (right) to cut patterns. Simply cut a template from particleboard or fiberboard, and mount it to the stock with double-faced carpet tape. Mount the bit in the router and adjust the depth of cut so the pilot bearing rubs against the edge of the template while the bit cuts the edge of the stock.

2-2   The tip of a pattern-cutting bit cuts, making it a good choice for routing inside shapes, such as the cut-out in this oval frame. To keep from routing through your workbench, place a piece of plywood under the workpiece.

2-3   A pattern-cutting bit is also a good choice for cutting contoured grooves, shaped mortises, and cut-in decorations — such as these linked circles — that don't go all the way through the stock. Note that the template for routing the circles isn't all one piece. It consists of several parts that are fastened to the stock individually.

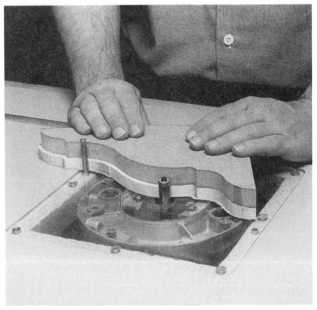

2-4   When cutting completely through the stock, a flush-trim bit in a table-mounted router is usually your safest choice. You have a good view of the template and the work-piece as you work. Cut away *most* of the material with a band saw or scroll saw, then remove the last $1/8$ to $1/4$ inch of stock with the router.

2-5   Although you can't cut with the tip of a flush-trim bit, you can still use it to make inside cuts. After mounting the template to the stock, drill a hole in the waste slightly larger than the diameter of the bit. Carefully lower the hole over the bit and begin cutting.

Take care when making pattern routing templates. Use a dense, stable material, such as particleboard or MDF (medium density fiberboard). When you lay out the template, remember that the radii of the inside curves should be no less than the diameter of the bit. If the template includes a sharp inside corner, the bit won't cut it — the corner will be left rounded on the inside. Cut the template with a band saw or scroll saw, then carefully sand and file the edges to remove the saw marks. Also make sure that the curves are "fair" — that is, there are no flat spots. Because the piloted bit follows the template precisely, it will reproduce any mistakes or irregularities.

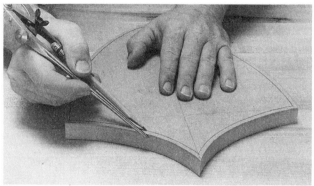

2-6 Because the diameter of the guide collar doesn't often match the cutting diameter of the router bit, the template must be a different size than the pattern you wish to rout. Usually, the collar is larger than the bit. When this is the case, lay out the pattern you want to rout on the template stock and cut it on the band saw or scroll saw. Sand the sawed edges. Subtract the diameter of the bit from the diameter of the guide collar and divide the difference by 2. For example, if you're using a $^5/_8$-inch-diameter guide collar and a $^1/_2$-inch-diameter bit, half the difference is $^1/_{16}$ inch:

$$(^5/_8 - ^1/_2) \div 2 = ^1/_{16}.$$

Set a compass divider to $^1/_{16}$ inch. Using the metal point to trace the contoured edge of the template, scribe a line parallel to the edge and $^1/_{16}$ inch *inside* it.

TRY THIS TRICK

Want to reproduce a shape quickly and precisely *without* going through the trouble of making a template? Use an existing part to make copies. Adhere the shaped part to the stock with double-faced carpet tape. Using either a pattern-cutting or a flush-trim bit, cut the stock while tracing the shaped part with the bearing. **Note:** Remember, the router bit won't cut inside corners that are smaller than the bit diameter. You'll have to cut these with a band saw or scroll saw.

PATTERN ROUTING WITH A GUIDE COLLAR

A guide collar, used in conjunction with an unpiloted bit, allows you to rout a pattern in much the same way as with a piloted straight bit — the collar follows the shape of the template, while the bit cuts the pattern. There are some important differences, however. With a few exceptions, a guide collar can be mounted on a hand-held router only. And because the diameter of the guide collar is usually a different size than the cutting diameter of the bit, the template must be a different size than the pattern you wish to cut. (*SEE FIGURES 2-6 AND 2-7.*)

Although it requires more figuring to make a pattern routing template for a guide collar than it does to make one for a piloted straight bit, this technique has an important advantage. You aren't confined to using only straight bits — you can rout patterns with a wide variety of unpiloted router bits, including dovetail, core-box, beading, V-groove, and roundnose bits. (*SEE FIGURE 2-8.*)

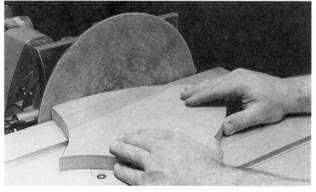

2-7 Using a scroll saw with a fine blade, saw along the line you have scribed to cut the template to the proper size. Or, if you must remove just a little material, sand the template to the proper size with a disk sander, a drum sander, or files.

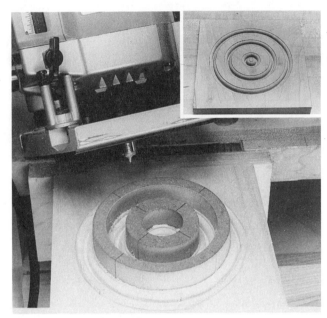

2-8 Using a guide collar to follow a template gives you the flexibility to rout with almost any *unpiloted* router bit. This, in turn, lets you cut patterned grooves and mortises with shaped sides and bottoms. For example, the corner molding shown was routed with a beading bit to round the top edges of the groove. You can also use dovetail, round-nose, core-box, and V-groove bits, as well as ordinary straight bits.

PIN ROUTING

You can also reproduce the shape of a template by pin routing. Mount a short, sturdy metal rod or *pin* directly above or below an unpiloted router bit, and align the center of the pin with the center of the bit. Attach a template to one side of a *spacer* (a scrap of plywood), and the workpiece to the other side. Slide this assembly horizontally, tracing the shape of the template with the pin while the bit cuts the workpiece. (*SEE FIGURES 2-9 THROUGH 2-11.*)

TRY THIS TRICK

To pin rout small patterns, make the spacer much larger than the template. Hold on to the spacer as you trace the template with the pin. This will keep your fingers a safe distance from the router bit.

This pattern routing technique combines many of the advantages of a piloted straight bit and a guide collar. If you use a straight bit and a pin that are the same diameter, you can make the template the same size as the shape you want to rout — just as you do when using a piloted straight bit. However, you aren't limited to straight bits. You can pin rout with a variety of unpiloted bits, as you can when working with a guide collar.

FOR YOUR INFORMATION

Many commercial sign-making kits rely on the guide collar pattern routing technique. The letters and numbers are individual templates, all the same size and all designed to work with the same guide collar. To make words and numerals, place the templates in a frame one at a time, position them over the stock, and rout them.

2-9 To pin rout a pattern, position the pin just below or just above the router bit and align them. Make a template and glue this to one face of a spacer — a scrap of plywood slightly larger than the template and ¼ to ½ inch thick. Attach the stock that you wish to rout to the other face with double-faced carpet tape. When you rout, the edge of the template will ride against the pin. As it does, the bit cuts the template shape in the workpiece. **Warning:** If you use nails or screws to attach either the template or the workpiece to the spacer, carefully position these fasteners so the bit won't nick them when you rout.

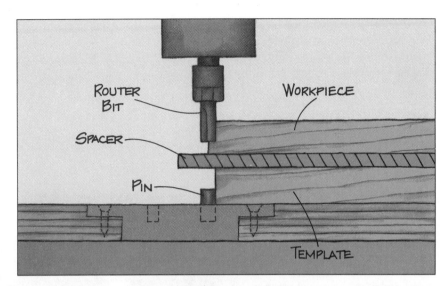

2-10 To set up for a cut, first adjust the depth of cut so the router bit will not cut the stock. If the pin is mounted above the router, lower the bit so the tip is below the table. If the pin is below the router, as shown, raise the bit above the workpiece. Place the assembled template, spacer, and workpiece so the pin rests against the edge of the template. Holding the assembly firmly with one hand, turn on the router and readjust the depth of cut so the bit cuts ⅛ to ¼ inch into the workpiece. Slide the workpiece horizontally, tracing the shape of the template with the pin as the bit cuts.

2-11 After finishing one pass, readjust the depth of cut another ⅛ to ¼ inch deeper and make another pass. Repeat until you can cut the pattern as deep as necessary. If you wish to cut all the way through the workpiece, adjust the depth of cut on your last pass so the bit cuts into (but not through) the spacer. After routing, remove the workpiece from the spacer. **Warning:** If the pin is overhead and the workpiece covers the bit, be especially careful as you adjust the depth of cut. You don't want your hands in harm's way if the spinning bit pokes up through the stock.

If there is a disadvantage to pin routing, it's that it requires more equipment than any other pattern routing technique. You must build or purchase a fixture that holds either a router over a pin or a pin over a router. There are three common choices:

■ Purchase an overarm router.
■ Make an overhead routing jig and a pin block.
■ Make an overarm pin holder. (*See Figures 2-12 through 2-14.*)

2-12 There are three different fixtures you can use to pin rout. The easiest to use is an *overarm router.* This commercial tool suspends a router motor above a *pin block* — a metal socket in the worktable that holds several different sizes of pins. A mechanism raises and lowers the motor several inches and locks it in any vertical position within that range. This makes it simple to adjust the depth of cut. The drawback to an overarm router is its expense. However, you may be able to justify the cost when you consider that, in addition to pin routing, this tool will also perform all the operations you can do on a table-mounted router. If you do a lot of pattern routing, consider replacing a router table with an overarm router.

2-13 The least expensive fixture (and the easiest to make) for pin routing is a shopmade *overhead routing jig.* Mount a *plunge router* on the jig, fasten the jig to a workbench or router table, and use a *height adjustor* to set the depth of cut. To hold the pins under the router, either make a hardwood pin block or drill holes in the bench or table top. This simple setup will perform many of the same operations as an overarm router, but the size of the patterns that you can pin rout is limited. For plans on how to make an overhead routing jig, see the Router Workbench on page 103. You can purchase a height adjustor accessory for most plunge routers, or you can make your own following the plans in "Pin Routing Accessories" on the facing page.

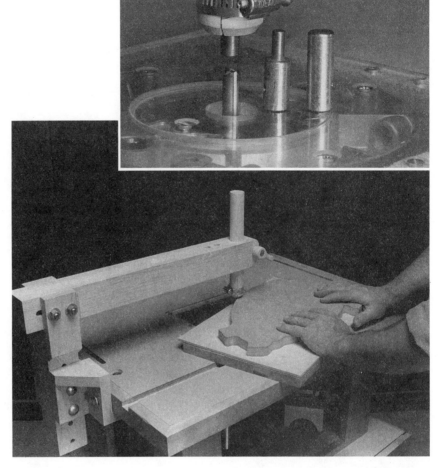

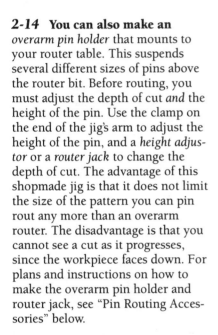

2-14 You can also make an *overarm pin holder* that mounts to your router table. This suspends several different sizes of pins above the router bit. Before routing, you must adjust the depth of cut *and* the height of the pin. Use the clamp on the end of the jig's arm to adjust the height of the pin, and a *height adjustor* or a *router jack* to change the depth of cut. The advantage of this shopmade jig is that it does not limit the size of the pattern you can pin rout any more than an overarm router. The disadvantage is that you cannot see a cut as it progresses, since the workpiece faces down. For plans and instructions on how to make the overarm pin holder and router jack, see "Pin Routing Accessories" below.

PIN ROUTING ACCESSORIES

You can pin rout on an ordinary router table, provided you make several simple accessories. First, you must have an *overarm pin holder* to suspend the pin above the router bit. This jig mounts to either the back or the side edge of the tabletop. Calculate the length of the arm so the pin holder can be positioned directly over the router bit. Fasten the mounting bracket to the router table with carriage bolts through the mount and lag screws through the ledger. Counterbore the bolt holes so the heads of the bolts will be flush with or slightly below the surface of the table.

You must also devise a safe way to adjust the router's depth of cut *with one hand* while the router is running. This is so you can hold the workpiece

and template down on the table with the other hand as you raise the spinning bit into the wood. There are two simple ways to make a one-handed depth of cut adjustment. If you're using a plunge router, outfit the tool with a *height adjustor.* This accessory fits over the threaded post, replacing the stop nuts that help control the vertical position of the router. If you're using an ordinary router, you can adjust the depth of cut with a *router jack.* The jig fits under the router, raising and lowering the motor as you turn the knob. The knob is mounted on a standard 3/8-inch-diameter, coarse-threaded carriage bolt. The thread pitch (threads per inch) of this bolt is 16, so each counterclockwise turn of the knob raises the router motor exactly 1/16 inch.

(continued) ▷

PIN ROUTING ACCESSORIES — CONTINUED

1 **Before you can use the**
overarm pin holder, you must center
the pin over the bit. To do this, mount
a straight bit in the router and a pin of
equal diameter in the pin holder. Raise
the bit and lower the pin until the
two almost touch. Then loosen the
carriage bolts that hold the mounting bracket to the router table and
the arm to the post. Slide the arm
and the mounting bracket back and
forth until the pin is directly above
the bit. Check the alignment with a
small, square wood block. When
you're certain the pin and bit are
properly aligned, tighten the bolts.

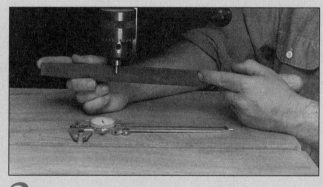

2 **After aligning the bit and**
pin, raise the pin to its working height
— it must clear the workpiece and the
spacer, but rub against the edges of
the template. Ordinarily, you should
be able to do this by loosening the
handle that secures the pin holder in
the arm and sliding the holder up or
down. However, if you need to raise
or lower the pin farther than the
length of the pin holder will allow,
remove the carriage bolts that hold
the post in the lower brackets, slide
the post up or down, and replace the
carriage bolts. **Note:** Keep the arm as
close to the template as possible. The
higher the arm and the further the
pin holder is extended down from
the arm, the less stable the pin is.

3 **The *shaft* of each pin — the**
portion that mounts in the pin holder
— must be $1/2$ inch in diameter. However, the pin itself can be any diameter you need. To make a pin, cut a
piece of $1/2$-inch metal rod $1 1/2$ inches
long. Mount this in the chuck of a
drill press. Turn the drill press on at
low speed and hold a file against the
lower $1/2$ inch of the rod, as shown.
As you file away the surface of the
rod, it will decrease in diameter and
form a pin. Every so often, check the
progress of your work with calipers.
When the pin is the proper size, stop
filing. To mount the pin, insert the
shaft in the hole at the bottom of the
pin holder and tighten the hose clamp.

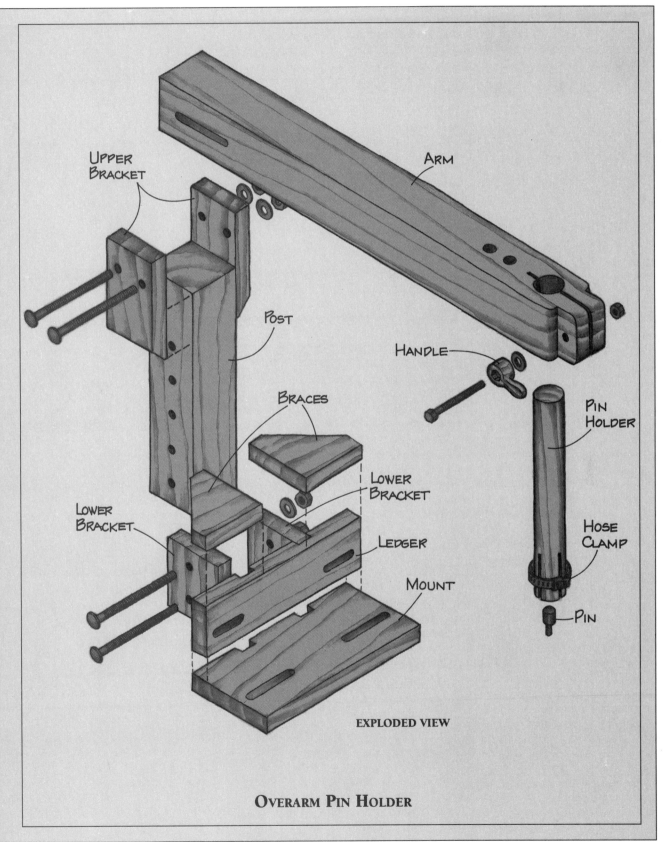

UPPER
BRACKET

ARM

POST

HANDLE

PIN
HOLDER

BRACES

LOWER
BRACKET

LEDGER

LOWER
BRACKET

HOSE
CLAMP

MOUNT

PIN

EXPLODED VIEW

OVERARM PIN HOLDER

(continued) ▷

Pin Routing Accessories — continued

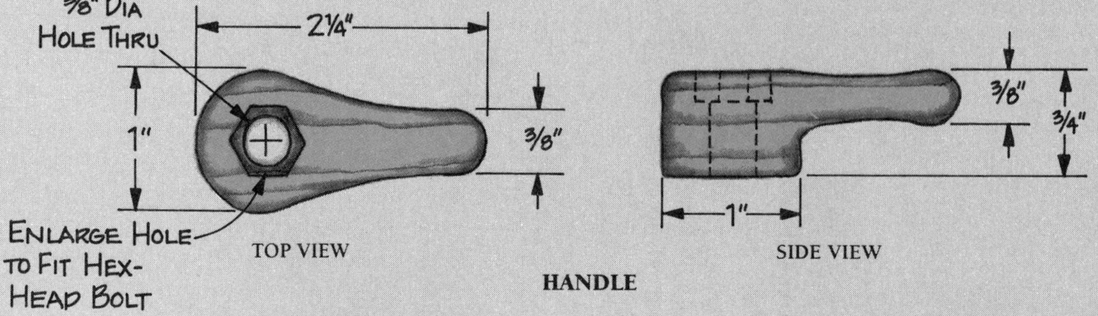
3/8" Dia Hole Thru
2¼"
1"
3/8"
Enlarge Hole to Fit Hex-Head Bolt
3/8"
3/4"
1"

TOP VIEW

SIDE VIEW

HANDLE

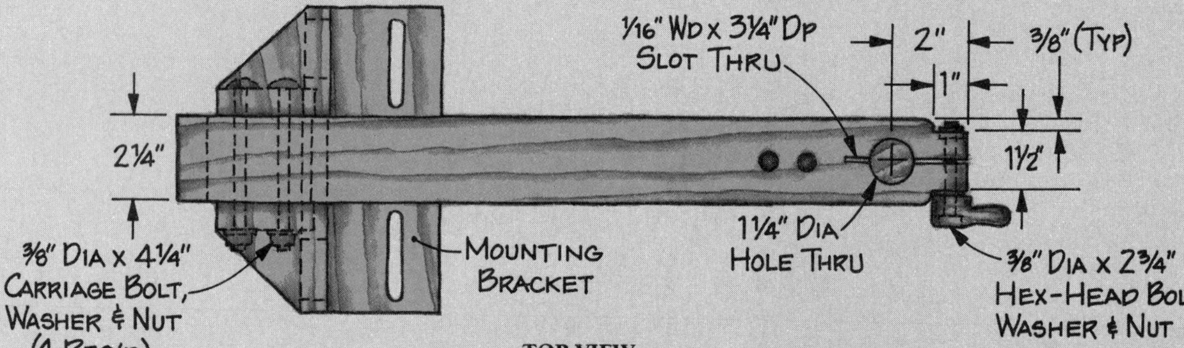
2¼"
3/8" Dia x 4¼" Carriage Bolt, Washer & Nut (4 Req'd)
Mounting Bracket
1/16" Wd x 3¼" Dp Slot Thru
2"
1"
3/8" (Typ)
1½"
1¼" Dia Hole Thru
3/8" Dia x 2¾" Hex-Head Bolt, Washer & Nut

TOP VIEW

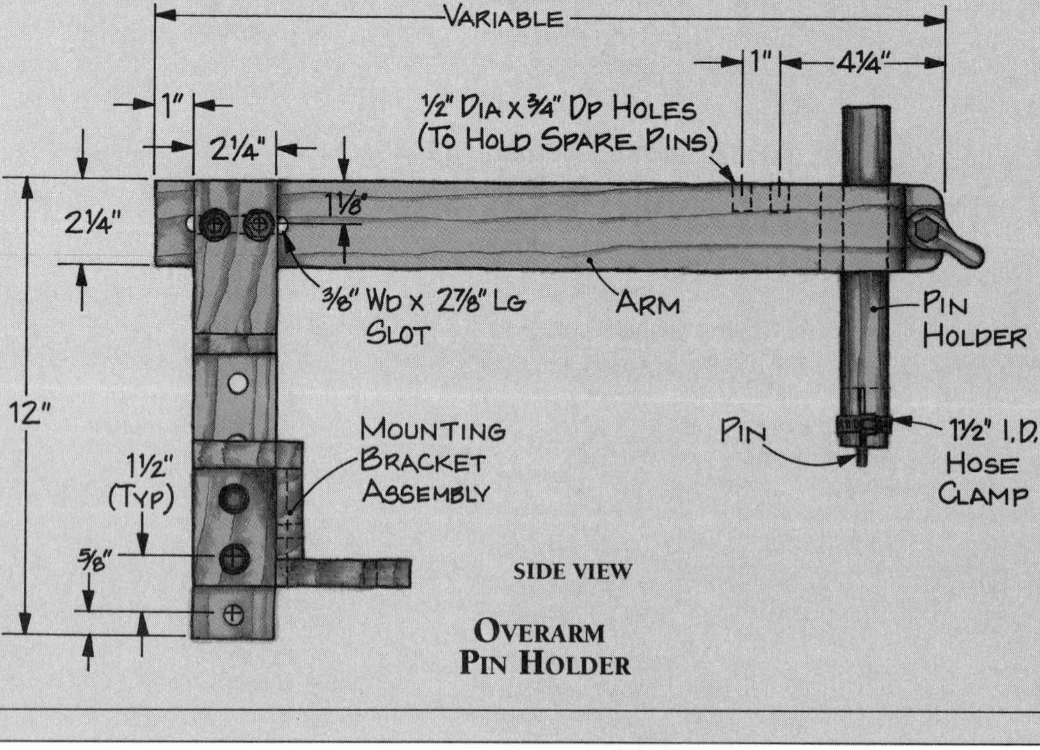
Variable
1"
4¼"
1"
2¼"
1/2" Dia x 3/4" Dp Holes (To Hold Spare Pins)
2¼"
1⅛"
3/8" Wd x 2⅞" Lg Slot
Arm
Pin Holder
12"
1½" (Typ)
5/8"
Mounting Bracket Assembly
Pin
1½" I.D. Hose Clamp

SIDE VIEW

Overarm Pin Holder

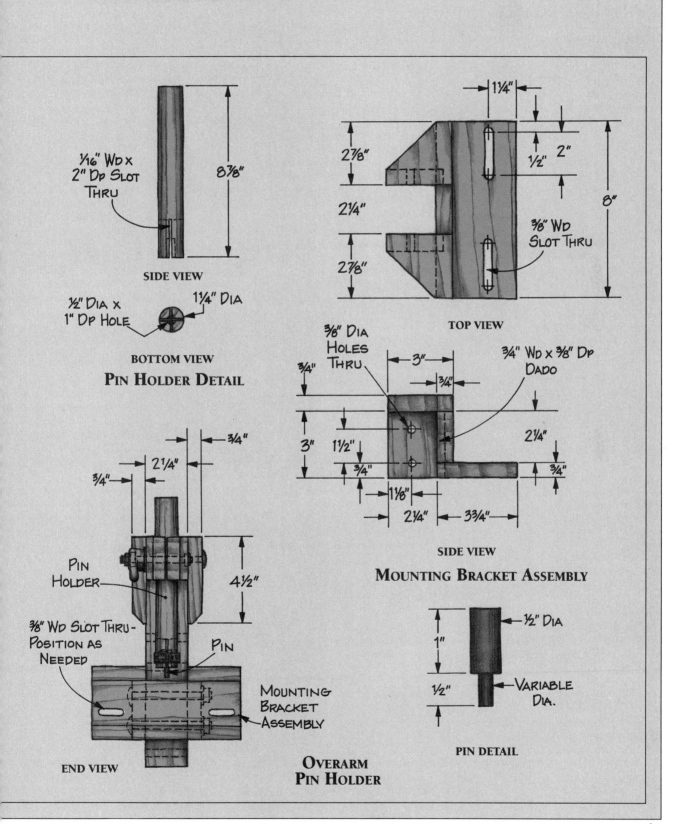

¹⁄₁₆" Wᴅ x
2" Dᴘ Sʟᴏᴛ
Tʜʀᴜ

8⅞"

SIDE VIEW

½" Dɪᴀ x
1" Dᴘ Hᴏʟᴇ

1¼" Dɪᴀ

BOTTOM VIEW
PIN HOLDER DETAIL

1¼"

2⅞"

½"   2"

8"

2¼"

2⅞"

⅜" Wᴅ
Sʟᴏᴛ Tʜʀᴜ

TOP VIEW

⅜" Dɪᴀ
Hᴏʟᴇs
Tʜʀᴜ

3"

¾"

¾"   ¾"

3"   1½"

2¼"

¾"

¾"

1⅛"

2¼"   3¾"

SIDE VIEW
MOUNTING BRACKET ASSEMBLY

¾"

2¼"

¾"

Pɪɴ
Hᴏʟᴅᴇʀ

4½"

⅜" Wᴅ Sʟᴏᴛ Tʜʀᴜ-
Pᴏsɪᴛɪᴏɴ ᴀs
Nᴇᴇᴅᴇᴅ

Pɪɴ

MOUNTING
BRACKET
ASSEMBLY

END VIEW

**OVERARM
PIN HOLDER**

½" Dɪᴀ

1"

½"

Vᴀʀɪᴀʙʟᴇ
Dɪᴀ.

PIN DETAIL

(continued) ▷

Pin Routing Accessories — continued

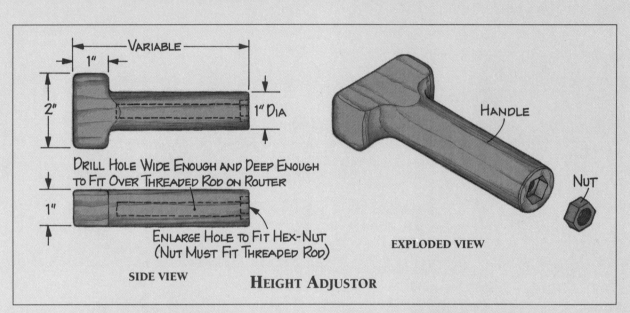

VARIABLE

1"

2"

1" DIA

DRILL HOLE WIDE ENOUGH AND DEEP ENOUGH
TO FIT OVER THREADED ROD ON ROUTER

1"

ENLARGE HOLE TO FIT HEX-NUT
(NUT MUST FIT THREADED ROD)

SIDE VIEW

HANDLE

NUT

EXPLODED VIEW

HEIGHT ADJUSTOR

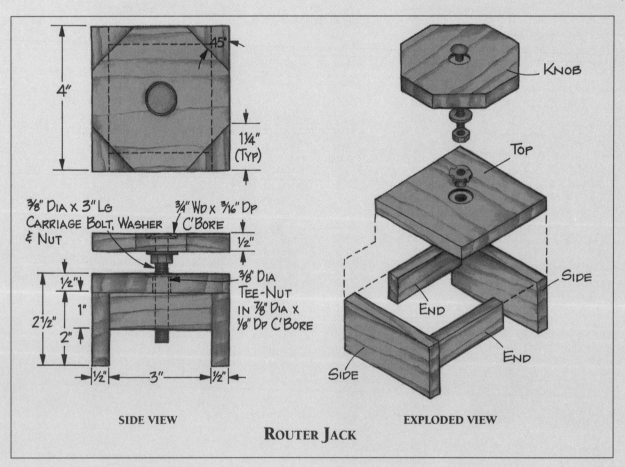

45°

4"

1¼"
(TYP)

⅜" DIA x 3" LG
CARRIAGE BOLT, WASHER
& NUT

¾" WD x 3/16" DP
C'BORE

½"

½"

1"

2½"

2"

⅜" DIA
TEE-NUT
IN ⅞" DIA x
⅛" DP C'BORE

½"   3"   ½"

SIDE VIEW

KNOB

TOP

SIDE

END

END

SIDE

EXPLODED VIEW

ROUTER JACK

SPECIAL PATTERN ROUTING TECHNIQUES

There are several useful pattern routing techniques that don't use templates, but require special jigs instead. For example, you can rout any pattern, from a simple shape to a detailed drawing, by mounting a router on a pantograph, then tracing the pattern with the pantograph's stylus. Or, you can rout perfect circles and ovals by controlling the router with a beam compass or trammel. You can even copy three-dimensional shapes, such as cabriole legs or carved moldings, using a router duplicator.

ROUTING CIRCLES

Cutting a circle is, perhaps, the simplest of all pattern routing operations. Use a straight bit to cut the wood, and swing the router (or the workpiece) around a *pivot* — the center of the circle. The distance between the pivot and the inside cutting edge (the edge closest to the pivot) determines the radius of the routed circle. The farther the distance from the pivot to the bit, the larger the circle will be.

Circles that are smaller than a router base must be cut with a table-mounted router. Make an auxiliary work surface to fit over the router table, then drive a screw up through this surface so it protrudes ¼ to ½ inch. This screw will serve as a pivot. Position the work surface on the router table so the pivot screw is the proper distance from the router bit, then clamp it in place. Rotate the stock on the pivot as the router bit cuts it. (*SEE FIGURES 2-15 AND 2-16.*)

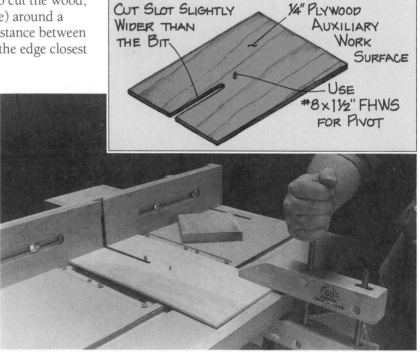

CUT SLOT SLIGHTLY WIDER THAN THE BIT.

¼" PLYWOOD AUXILIARY WORK SURFACE

USE #8 x 1½" FHWS FOR PIVOT

2-15 To make a simple circle-cutting jig for your router table, begin with an auxiliary work surface of ¼-inch plywood. Cut a blind groove in the plywood so the router bit can protrude through it, and drive a flathead screw through the plywood near the blind end of the groove. This will serve as a pivot. Place the jig on the router table and adjust its position so the distance from the pivot screw to the nearest edge of the straight bit is equal to the radius of the circle you wish to cut. Clamp the jig to the router table, or, if the clamps would interfere with the work, attach the jig to the table with double-faced carpet tape.

2-16 Drill a small hole in the underside of the workpiece and fit this hole over the pivot. Holding the stock down with a push block, turn the router on and raise the bit with a height adjustor or router jack until it cuts ⅛ to ¼ inch into the wood. Turn the workpiece one revolution on the pivot, then raise the bit another ⅛ to ¼ inch and repeat. Continue until the bit cuts completely through the wood.

You can rout larger circles with either a table-mounted or hand-held router. If you use a table-mounted router, there is a practical limit to the size of the circle you can make since the router table is only so large — you don't want to cut stock that is too big for the table to safely support. If the circle is larger than your router table, a hand-held router works best. Make an elongated sole or a beam that mounts to the base of a router. (SEE FIGURES 2-17 AND 2-18.) Both of these setups swing the router around a pivot like a beam compass or trammel. Plans for a circle-routing trammel jig are shown in "Trammel Jig" on page 45.

A SAFETY REMINDER

When cutting small pieces on a router table, be careful to keep your hands and fingers clear of the bit. You may wish to secure the stock to a push block or a large scrap with double-faced carpet tape to rout it safely.

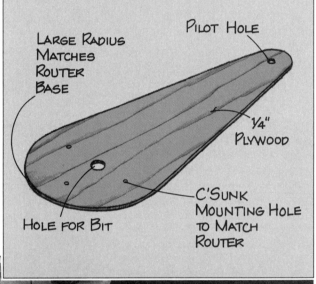

LARGE RADIUS MATCHES ROUTER BASE

PILOT HOLE

¼" PLYWOOD

HOLE FOR BIT

C'SUNK MOUNTING HOLE TO MATCH ROUTER

2-17 You can make a circle-cutting jig by cutting an elongated sole for your router from a scrap of ¼-inch plywood. Remove the plastic sole from your router and mount the plywood sole in its place. Drill a pivot hole through the sole the proper distance from the bit. Drive a small nail into the underside of the workpiece at the center of the circle you wish to rout. Hook the pivot hole over the nail, then swing the router around it as you cut.

For **B**est **R**esults

When cutting circles on a router table or with a hand-held router, don't try to cut through thick boards in one step. Cut the circle in several passes, cutting ⅛ to ¼ inch deeper with each pass. For hand-held operations, a plunge router makes it easy to feed the bit into the wood in increments. When working with a router table, use a *height adjustor* or *router jack* to feed the bit. Plans for these two shopmade accessories are shown in "Pin Routing Accessories" on page 35.

ROUTING OVALS

While circles have a constant radius, ovals don't. The radius of an oval (or *ellipse*) is greatest along the major axis (the length of the oval), and smallest along the minor axis (the width). Ovals also have two pivot points, each of which is called a *focus*. (*SEE FIGURE 2-19.*)

The technique for routing an oval relies on the same principle as routing a circle, but you must swing the router around *both* pivots or foci. To do this, make a *double trammel* — a beam compass with two moving pivots — on which to mount the router. (See the "Trammel Jig" on page 45 for plans and instructions.) This jig works in the same fashion as a smoke grinder, a folk toy with a crank handle that describes an ellipse as you turn it. (*SEE FIGURES 2-20 THROUGH 2-22.*) By substituting a router for the handle, you can rout perfect ovals.

2-18 If you wish to avoid drilling a hole or driving a nail into the workpiece to make a pivot, you can make a detachable pivot by driving a screw, nail, or bolt up through a block of wood. Use double-faced carpet tape to attach this pivot block to the workpiece over the center of the circle you want to rout. Mount the router on the end of a beam, hook the beam over the pivot, and swing the router around it while cutting the workpiece. **Note:** The router mount at the end of the beam must be offset to compensate for the thickness of the pivot block.

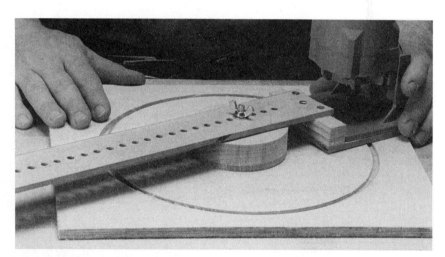

2-19 Ovals have two axes, major (length) and minor (width), which cross at point Y. The oval shape revolves around two pivots or *foci* (A and B), which are positioned along the major axis. The shape of the oval is determined by how far apart the foci are (AB). The farther apart, the more elongated the oval will appear — the minor axis (EF) will become much smaller in relation to the major axis (CD). The size of the oval is determined by the distance from one focus to the oval's edge, along the major axis (AC or BD).

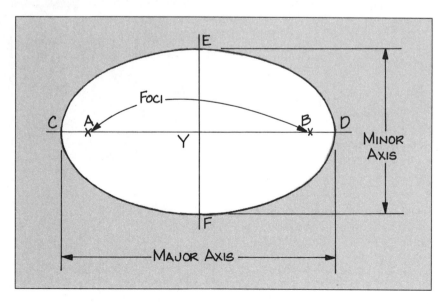

2-20 Before you rout an oval with a double trammel, decide the length of the major and minor axes, then mark them on the workpiece. Center the double trammel pivot block over the point where the major and minor axes cross (Y), aligning one sliding pivot with the major axis and the other with the minor axis. Stick the pivot block to the workpiece with double-faced carpet tape. Mount the router on the beam, align with the major axis, and position the router so the bit is at one end of that axis. Center the minor pivot (the pivot that moves along the minor axis) over point Y and fasten the beam to it.

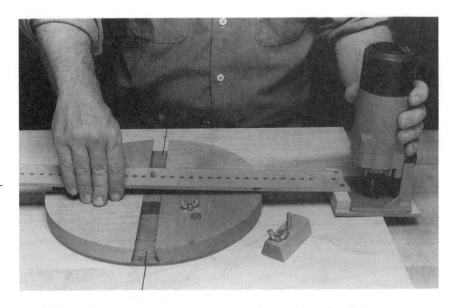

2-21 Swing the beam 90 degrees, aligning it with the minor axis, and position the router so the bit is at the end of that axis. Center the major pivot over point Y and fasten the beam to it. The beam should now be fastened to *both* pivots. To check the setup, swing the router once around the pivots with the power *off*. The bit should pass over the ends of the major and minor axes.

2-22 To cut the oval with the double trammel, swing the router around the pivots, pulling *gently* outward. This slight tension will take any play out of the mechanical system as the pivots slide back and forth in their grooves.

TRAMMEL JIG

This fixture enables you to rout *both* circles and ovals of different sizes. The router is attached to a beam, which can be fastened to two different pivots. When attached to a single fixed pivot, it works like an ordinary beam compass or *trammel*, allowing you to rout circles. When fastened to a double sliding pivot, it becomes a *double trammel* so you can rout ovals. Holes in the beam, spaced every ½ inch, allow you to adjust the distance between the router and the pivot. This, in turn, lets you change the size of the circle, or the size and shape of the oval.

The fixed trammel pivot is just a block with a flathead machine bolt through the center. The sliding double-trammel pivot has two dovetail grooves at right angles to one another. A dovetail-shaped pivot block with a machine bolt through the center slides back and forth in each groove. The holes in the beam fit over these bolts.

Note: You can rout circles from 6 inches up to 60 inches in diameter with the simple trammel setup. The double trammel, however, is more limited. As shown, you can rout ovals with a minimum minor axis of 12 inches and a maximum major axis of 48 inches. The difference between the major and minor axes must be no more than 12 inches. If you need to rout an oval that doesn't fall within these parameters, you will have to make a smaller or larger sliding pivot.

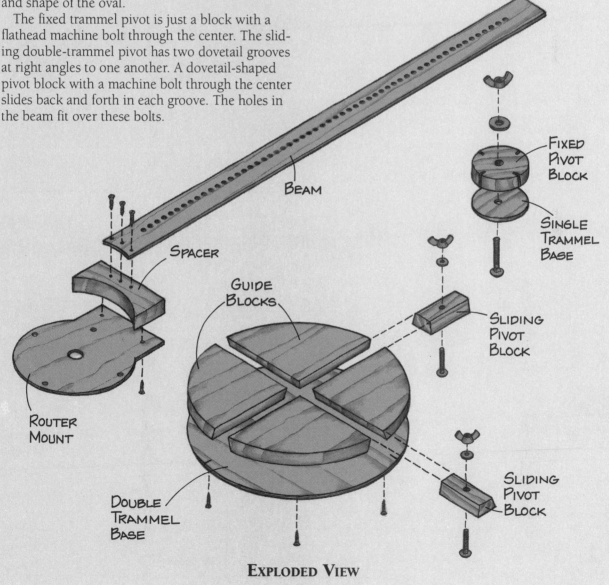

BEAM

FIXED PIVOT BLOCK

SINGLE TRAMMEL BASE

SPACER

GUIDE BLOCKS

SLIDING PIVOT BLOCK

ROUTER MOUNT

DOUBLE TRAMMEL BASE

SLIDING PIVOT BLOCK

EXPLODED VIEW

(continued) ▷

TRAMMEL JIG — CONTINUED

1 **Mount both the trammel**
and the double-trammel pivots on the
workpiece with double-faced carpet
tape. To position the trammel pivot,
mark the center of the circle with
lines that cross at 90 degrees. The
length of these lines should be longer
than the diameter of the pivot. Then
align the marks on the edge of the
pivot with these crossed lines. The
procedure is the same for locating
the double-trammel pivot, but use
the layout lines on the workpiece that
mark the major and minor axes. Note
that the alignment marks on the
double-trammel pivot are centered at
the ends of the dovetail grooves. This
ensures that the sliding pivots will be
aligned with the axes.

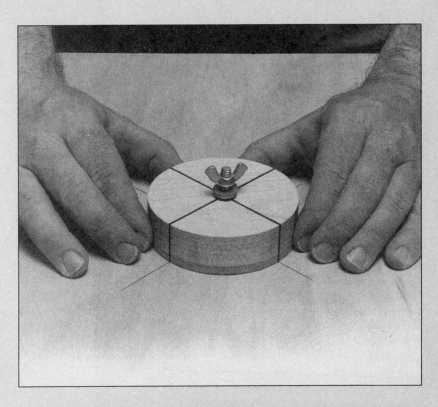

2 **Although you can mount**
any size of router to the end of the
beam, small routers are easier to
"swing" — rotate around the pivot.
The trammel jig shown mounts a
laminate trimmer. **Note:** If you want
to use more than one router with this
jig, don't fasten the mount to the
beam permanently. Instead, make a
mount for each router and screw (but
don't glue) these to the beam.

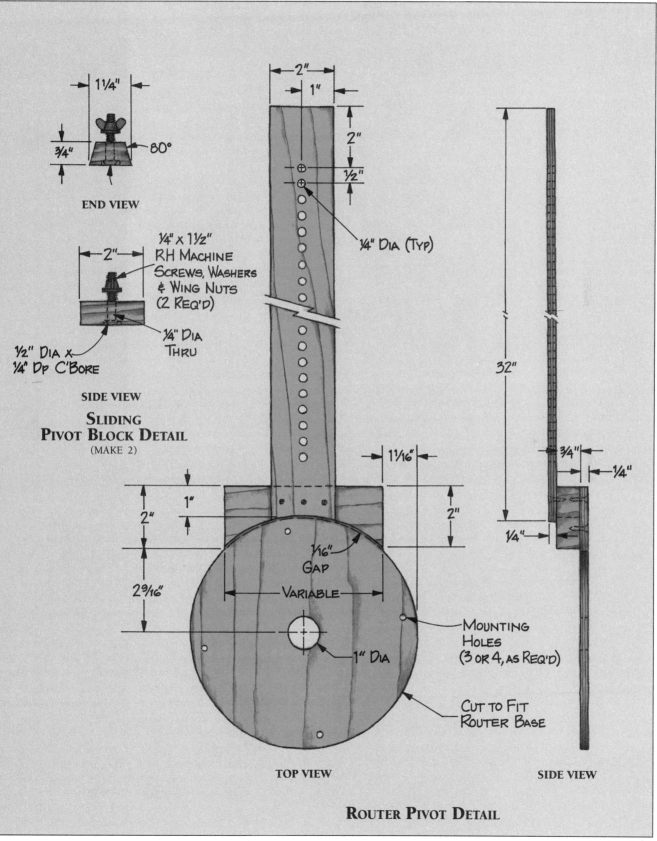

1¼"

¾"

80°

END VIEW

2"

¼" x 1½"
RH Machine
Screws, Washers
& Wing Nuts
(2 Req'd)

½" Dia x
¼" Dp C'Bore

¼" Dia
Thru

SIDE VIEW

**Sliding
Pivot Block Detail**
(MAKE 2)

2"

1"

2"

½"

¼" Dia (Typ)

1¹⁄₁₆"

1"

2"

2"

2⁹⁄₁₆"

1⁄₁₆"
Gap

Variable

1" Dia

Mounting
Holes
(3 or 4, as Req'd)

Cut to Fit
Router Base

TOP VIEW

32"

¾"

¼"

¼"

SIDE VIEW

Router Pivot Detail

(continued) ▷

TRAMMEL JIG — CONTINUED

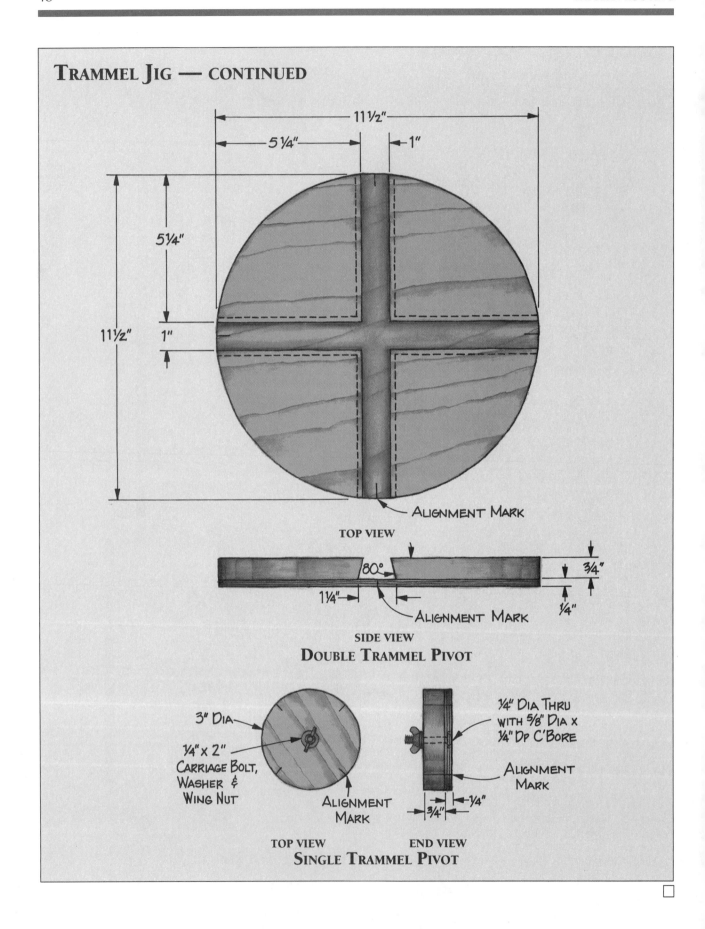

ALIGNMENT MARK

TOP VIEW

ALIGNMENT MARK

SIDE VIEW
DOUBLE TRAMMEL PIVOT

3" DIA

¼" x 2"
CARRIAGE BOLT,
WASHER &
WING NUT

ALIGNMENT
MARK

¼" DIA THRU
WITH ⅝" DIA x
¼" DP C'BORE

ALIGNMENT
MARK

TOP VIEW   **END VIEW**
SINGLE TRAMMEL PIVOT

ROUTING WITH A PANTOGRAPH

A pantograph is a drafting tool that enlarges or reduces plans and patterns. It consists of four beams joined together to make a flexible parallelogram. One corner of the parallelogram is anchored, the opposite corner is fitted with a stylus, and a pencil can be mounted somewhere in between. As you trace a shape with the stylus, the pencil draws an enlarged or reduced copy.

Several tool manufacturers have adapted the pantograph, substituting a router for the pencil. As you trace a drawing or a layout with the stylus, the router cuts a scaled copy. Most router pantographs are made to *reduce* patterns between 40 and 60 percent — it's much easier to control the router when each movement of the stylus produces a smaller movement of the router than it is the other way around. (*SEE FIGURES 2-23 AND 2-24.*)

Note: You can use almost any unpiloted router bit with a pantograph jig, including straight, roundnose, V-groove, beading, and core-box bits.

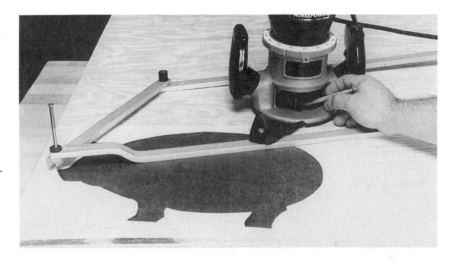

2-23 You can use a pantograph to reproduce *reduced* copies of patterns, including letters, numerals, shapes, and figures. Mount a router in the pantograph, then attach one corner of the pantograph to a sheet of plywood. Tape the pattern you want to reproduce to the plywood, under the stylus. With the router turned *off,* trace the outside shape of the pattern with the stylus. As you do so, mark the area that is encompassed by the movement of the router bit. Mount the stock you want to rout in this area.

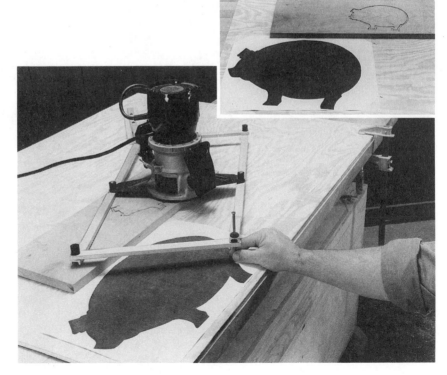

2-24 Adjust the router's depth of cut to rout $\frac{1}{8}$ to $\frac{1}{4}$ inch deep. Hold the router and pantograph above the workpiece (the anchor arm will flex slightly to allow you to do this), turn the router on, and carefully lower the tool onto the wood. As you do so, make sure the stylus lands on some portion of the pattern you wish to rout. Trace the entire pattern with the stylus. As you move the stylus, the router moves in the same direction, although a shorter distance. When you have finished tracing the pattern, the router will have cut a smaller copy of it in the workpiece. If you need to rout deeper, readjust the depth of cut to lower the bit another $\frac{1}{8}$ to $\frac{1}{4}$ inch, and repeat.

ROUTING THREE-DIMENSIONAL SHAPES

Just as you can trace the edge of a template with a pilot or a pin to duplicate two-dimensional shapes with a router, you can trace a surface to copy *three-*dimensional shapes. The trick is moving the router in all three dimensions.

There are several router accessories on the market that do just that. These *router duplicators* mount a router motor in a counterbalanced frame that allows it to travel side to side, up and down, and front to back. Furthermore, the motor can be tilted as it moves. Like the pantograph, these jigs have a movable stylus. As you move and tilt the stylus, the router bit follows its every movement. (*SEE FIGURE 2-25.*)

The most obvious application for a router duplicator is replicating wood carvings. However, this is only a fraction of what it can do. Many woodworkers use the jig to copy chair seats, cabriole legs, ball-and-claw feet, gun stocks, pegheads for musical instruments, ornate moldings, and similar three-dimensional shapes.

(*SEE FIGURES 2-26 THROUGH 2-28.*) It's also useful in repairing antiques, and it makes a passable lathe duplicator. (*SEE FIGURE 2-29.*) And if you have an artistic bent, you can use a duplicator freehand to rough out an original carving.

WHERE TO FIND IT

Router pantographs and duplicators are available from:

Wood Mizer Products
8180 West Tenth Street
Indianapolis, IN 46214

Sears, Roebuck, and Company
P.O. Box 7003
Downers Grove, IL 60515

2-25 A router duplicator is a large frame that lets you both move a router in all three dimensions and tilt it through a wide range of angles. The duplicator uses several interchangeable styluses and matching router bits — the end of each stylus is exactly the same shape as its companion bit. As you move a stylus over the surface of a three-dimensional shape, the router bit cuts a duplicate shape in the workpiece.

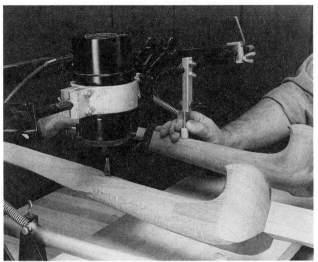

2-26 A duplicator is especially useful when you need to make a matched *set* of shaped pieces, such as the cabriole legs in a set of Queen Anne chairs. When duplicating these shapes, you'll need to do a little work on each workpiece before *and* after using the duplicator. Cut the rough shapes of all the legs on a band saw. Using hand tools, work the first leg to its final shape, then use this as a template for the remaining legs. Rough out the blanks with a large stylus and bit...

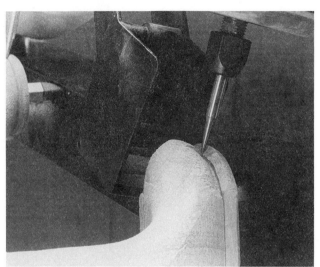

2-27 ...then switch to progressively smaller bits to cut smaller details, such as the pad of this cabriole foot. When cutting smooth shapes without small details, such as a chair seat, changing bits may be unnecessary.

2-28 After cutting the surfaces of each workpiece as smooth as you can with the router, clean up the shapes with hand tools and abrasives — spokeshaves, scrapers, files, and sanders.

2-29 The template does not have to be a finished workpiece, nor does it have to be made of wood. You can make a three-dimensional template from putty, clay, plaster, or any other easily worked material, then rout this shape in wood. Here, the missing parts of a broken molding have been filled in with wood putty and sanded smooth. This makes an adequate template for routing a replacement.

3

ROUTING AND LATHE TURNING

Using a router in conjunction with a lathe opens up a whole range of new turning possibilities. Traditional lathe tools are designed to cut *perpendicular* to the axis of a turning, but a router will cut *parallel* to the axis as well. For example, by drawing the router along the length of a spindle (cutting parallel to the axis), you can create reeds and flutes. Or, rotate the workpiece on a lathe and feed the router into it (cutting perpendicular to the axis) to make beads, coves, and grooves.

These operations are no more difficult than other routing procedures, but you must overcome a limitation in the design of the router. Routers are made to cut *flat* wooden surfaces. When rout-

ing an ordinary board, the base of the router rests flat on the stock and the stock rests flat on the workbench. A lathe turning, however, is a cylinder; the only flat spots are the ends. To rout a cylindrical workpiece, you must devise and build a special jig to hold either the router or the workpiece — or both.

ROUTING ALONG THE LENGTH OF A TURNING

To rout flutes, reeds, and similar shapes that run along the length of a turning, you must do three things:

■ Hold the turning so the same spot on the circumference always faces the router.

■ Guide the router parallel to the axis of rotation.

■ Rotate the turning a precise number of degrees between each cut to evenly space the cuts around the circumference. (SEE FIGURE 3-1.)

The lathe, of course, is designed to hold cylindrical stock, and you can take advantage of this when building a routing jig — use the lathe to hold the workpiece you want to rout, then erect a jig around it. Many craftsmen simply attach a platform to the lathe bed to hold the router above the turning. (SEE FIGURE 3-2.)

There are, however, problems with this approach. Most lathes do not provide a way to lock a turning so it cannot rotate; and only large, expensive lathes have "indexing heads" — mechanisms that allow you to rotate a turning a precise number of degrees. Oftentimes, it's less trouble to build a separate jig with built-in devices for locking and indexing than it is to try to adapt a lathe. (SEE FIGURE 3-3.)

No matter what approach you choose, the procedures for routing along the length of a turning are similar. First, adjust the fence or straightedge to guide the router so the bit remains *above the axis* all during

3-1 To space flutes, reeds, or other routed shapes evenly around a turning, you must be able to *index* it — that is, rotate it a precise amount. For example, if you want to rout 12 flutes, you must be able to rotate a turning $1/12$ of a turn, or 30 degrees. If you turn the stock 30 degrees after routing each flute, the flutes will be spaced evenly around the circumference of the turning.

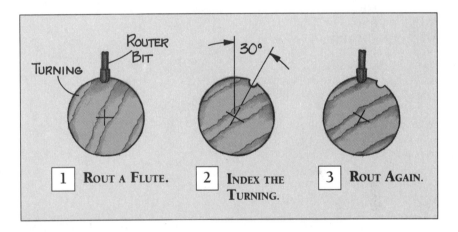

3-2 This large industrial lathe has an indexing head — a mechanism that will rotate a turning a precise number of degrees and lock it in place. To rout flutes, reeds, and other shapes parallel to the axis of rotation, simply attach a platform to the lathe to hold the router above the turning. Make the platform supports adjustable so you can raise and lower the router, and cut a groove down the middle of the platform to accommodate the router bit. Clamp a fence or a straightedge on the platform to guide the router.

the cut. (*SEE FIGURE 3-4.*) Place the router on the platform and against the fence, then adjust the depth of cut so the bit cuts into the turning. Remember, don't cut deeper than ¼ inch in a single pass. If you need to make a deep cut, plan to rout it in several passes. When you're satisfied with the setup, turn on the router, lower the bit into the workpiece, and make the cut. Keep the base of the router firmly against the fence as you work. (*SEE FIGURE 3-5.*)

FOR BEST RESULTS

When routing parallel to the axis of a turning, use a *plunge router* if you have one. The cuts that create reeds, flutes, and similar shapes are usually *blind* — they have a definite beginning and end. It's much easier to begin and end blind cuts with a plunge router than it is with a standard router.

3-3 If your lathe doesn't have an indexing head, you may wish to build a separate "fluting jig" to rout flutes and reeds. The jig shown holds a spindle turning, indexes it, and locks it in position. A platform with adjustable fences holds and guides the router above the turning. In one important respect, this shop-made jig is more versatile than an indexing lathe — you can make the indexing wheel so it rotates the turning any number of degrees you wish. (Most commercial indexing heads are designed to rotate the turning in 15-degree increments, period.) For plans and instructions on how to make this fixture, see the "Fluting Jig" on page 60.

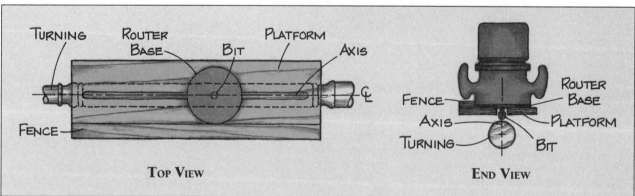

TOP VIEW   **END VIEW**

3-4 When routing flutes, reeds, and similar shapes, use a fence or straightedge to guide the router parallel to the axis of the turning. If the router does not travel parallel to that axis, the cut will not be straight and the depth of cut won't be uniform. In addition, the fence must guide the router so the bit is directly above the axis *all during the cut.* (If you draw an imaginary line through the center of the bit lengthwise, that line should be a *radial* of the turning — it must point directly at the axis of rotation.) If the bit is not directly above the axis, the cut won't be symmetrical; one side will be deeper than the other.

3-5 Once you have positioned the fence on the platform, adjust the router's depth of cut. If the bit won't cut deeply enough, lower the platform, raise the turning, or use a longer bit. Place the router on the platform where you want to begin cutting, holding the base firmly against the fence. Turn on the router, lower the bit into the wood, and begin the cut. In most cases, you'll want to feed the router from left to right as you face the fence — the rotation of the bit will help to hold the router against it. When you come to the end of the cut, turn off the router and raise the bit.

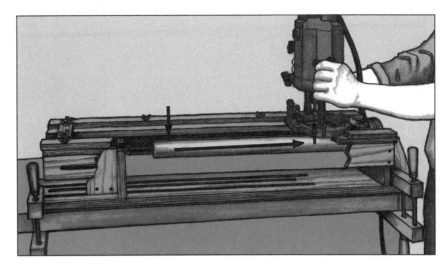

ROUTING REEDS AND FLUTES

When you lay out reeds and flutes, it's important to know the size of each reed or flute, as well as the space between them. First decide what bit you will use. Traditional reeds are normally made with point-cut (unpiloted) roundover bits, also called *beading bits*. Flutes are cut with *roundnose bits*. And you can use other unpiloted bits to create a variety of nontraditional shapes. (*See Figure 3-6.*)

Next, figure the spacing, in degrees, between each cut. Calculate the circumference of the turning by multiplying the diameter by *pi* (3.1416), and measure the *width* of the cut. If you're cutting reeds, the width of the cut will be equal to the *cutting* diameter of the beading bit. For flutes, the width will be equal to the cutting diameter of the roundnose bit *plus* the width

of the area you want to leave between each flute. Divide the circumference by the width of the cut to find how many cuts you must make. (If you come up with a fraction, round *down* to the nearest whole number.) Divide this number into 360 — the number of degrees in a full circle — to find the angular spacing between each cut. For example, if you wish to cut $\frac{1}{4}$-inch-wide flutes in a 2-inch-diameter turning, leaving about $\frac{1}{8}$ inch between each flute, you must cut 16 flutes:

$$(2 \times 3.1416) \div (\frac{1}{4} + \frac{1}{8}) = 16.7552$$

which rounds down to 16. The spacing between each flute should be $22\frac{1}{2}$ degrees:

$$360 \div 16 = 22\frac{1}{2}.$$

(*See Figure 3-7.*)

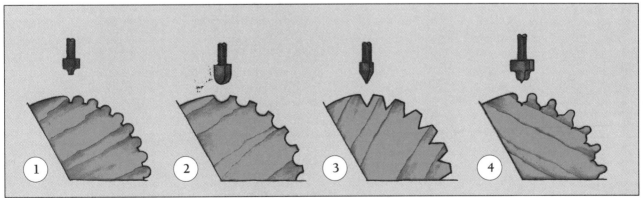

3-6 To cut traditional reeds in a spindle, use an unpiloted roundover bit or *beading bit* (1). For traditional flutes, use a *roundnose bit* (2). You can use many other unpiloted point-cut and top-cut router bits to create nontraditional shapes. A *V-groove bit* (3), for example, cuts a V-shaped flute. An unpiloted *ogee bit* (4) makes a combination reed and flute.

3-7 The spacing of reeds or flutes
around a lathe turning is ordinarily
figured in degrees rather than inches,
since the turnings must be indexed
in degrees. The number of degrees
from flute to flute (or reed to reed)
depends on the diameter of the turning, the width of the cuts, and the
width of any uncut space between
the cuts (1). As you increase the
diameter but keep the width of the
cuts and the uncut spaces the same,
the number of cuts increases and
the number of degrees between them
decreases (2). If you increase the
width of the cuts or the uncut spaces
but keep the diameter the same, the
number of cuts decreases and the
number of degrees between them
increases (3). If you increase both
the diameter and the widths propor-
tionately, the number of cuts and
degrees remains the same (4).

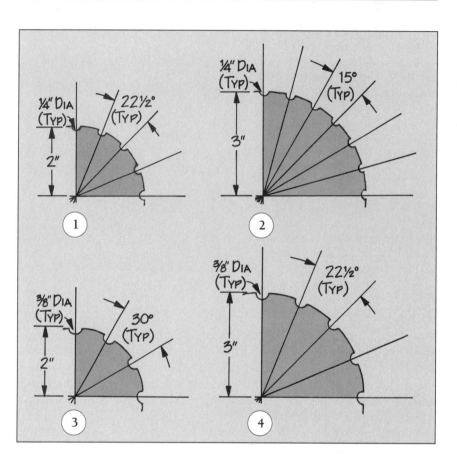

Do this figuring *before* you turn the workpiece. If
necessary, adjust the diameter of the turning to accommodate the size of the reeds or flutes that you
want to make. For example, if you want to cut 16
1/4-inch-wide flutes around a spindle, leaving *exactly*
1/8 inch between each of them, you should turn the
spindle to 1 29/32 inches in diameter:

$$[16 \times (1/4 + 1/8)] \div 3.1416 = 1^{29}/_{32}$$

without rounding up or down. You may also need to
adjust the size of the turning or the width of the cuts
because of the limitations of your jig. For example, if
you can index only 15 degrees with your setup, then
you cannot cut 16 flutes spaced 22 1/2 degrees apart.
You must cut either 12 flutes (30 degrees apart) or
24 (15 degrees apart). If you choose to cut 12 flutes,
then you must make either the flutes wider than 1/4
inch or the turning diameter smaller than 2 inches.
For 24 flutes, make the flutes narrower or the turning
larger.

Once you have figured the width of the cuts and
their spacing, mount the turning in the jig and position the fence to guide the router. It's also a good idea
to attach stop blocks to the jig's platform. These help
begin and end each cut in precisely the same location

so all the reeds or flutes will be precisely the same
length. Adjust the depth of cut and make the first cut.
Index the turning, rotating it the number of degrees
that you figured for the spacing between cuts. Make
the second cut and index the turning again. Repeat,
making evenly spaced cuts all around the circumference of the turning. (*SEE FIGURE 3-8.*)

FOR YOUR INFORMATION

When calculating the width of cut to make
reeds, remember that the *cutting* diameter of a
beading bit is not equal to its label. These bits are
labeled according to the radius that they cut. The
cutting diameter will be equal to twice this radius
plus the width of the *quirk* (the flat area between
the beads). For example, a 1/4-inch beading bit will
have a cutting diameter of slightly more than 1/2
inch. The easiest and most accurate way to find
this cutting diameter is to measure the bit with
calipers. Fortunately, you won't have this problem
when cutting flutes. The cutting diameter of a
roundnose bit *is* equal to its label.

3-8 To rout evenly spaced reeds or flutes around the circumference of a turning, you must index (rotate) the turning the same number of degrees before each cut. To keep the cuts the same length and to position them identically along the length of the turning, use stop blocks to begin and end each cut.

ROUTING TAPERED SPINDLES

The procedure for routing tapered spindles is essentially the same as for routing spindles of a uniform diameter, with some important exceptions.

To rout a tapered spindle, you must mount the workpiece so the surface closest to the platform is *parallel* to it. Otherwise, the cuts that you make won't be uniform in depth. To do this, one end of the spindle must be held at a different height than the other — the center of the smaller end must be higher or closer to the platform than the larger end. (SEE FIGURE 3-9.)

To calculate the difference in heights, subtract the diameter of the smaller end from that of the larger end and divide by 2. For example, to rout a spindle that tapers from 2 inches in diameter at one end to 1 inch at the other, the 1-inch-diameter end must be mounted ½ inch higher than the 2-inch-diameter end:
$$(2 - 1) \div 2 = \frac{1}{2}.$$

This simple calculation becomes much more difficult when only a portion of the spindle is tapered. If this is the case, it's easier to use a "feeler gauge" to help position the spindle. (SEE FIGURE 3-10.)

You must also consider that the cuts you make along the axis of a tapered spindle *won't* be parallel; they will grow farther apart at the wide end of the taper and closer together at the narrow end. This limits the shapes you can make. You may find it difficult to rout reeds, for example — these work best with parallel cuts. If you rout flutes, you must either increase the spacing or decrease the width of the cut so they don't merge at the narrow end of the taper.

3-9 To rout a tapered spindle, the surface closest to the platform (the surface to be routed) must be parallel to the platform. The distance from the platform to the spindle at the widest portion of the taper must be equal to the distance at the narrowest portion. To mount the spindle properly, the center of the narrow end must be higher than the wide end.

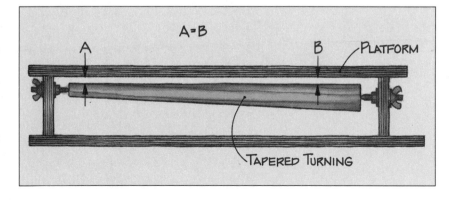

3-10 To help position a tapered
spindle in the fluting jig, use a combination square like a feeler gauge.
Mount the spindle in the jig and
place the square over the widest portion of the taper. Raise or lower the
straightedge so the tip just contacts
the spindle. Move the square over
the narrowest portion of the spindle
and raise the appropriate end of the
spindle until the surface contacts the
straightedge. To check the setup,
slide the square back and forth over
the tapered portion of the spindle —
the tip of the straightedge should
remain in contact with the surface
all along the taper.

TRY THIS TRICK

The setup used to rout tapered spindles can also
help you make small *pencil posts* — octagonal tapers
for table legs and bed posts. Use a wide straight bit to
form the sides of the octagon, indexing the spindle
45 degrees between each cut.

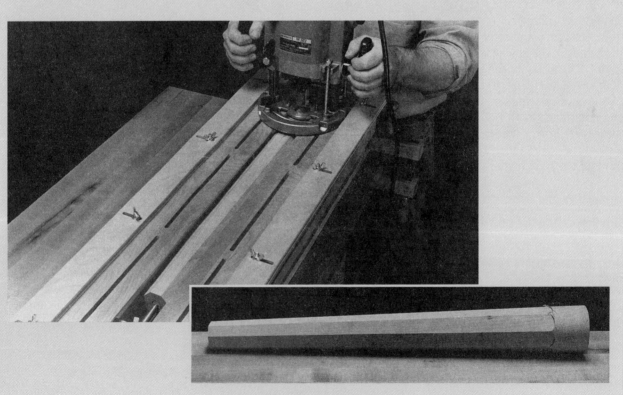

ROUTING SLOTS AND MORTISES

In addition to cutting decorative shapes along the axis of a turning, you can also use these techniques to cut joinery in cylindrical stock. To make a mortise in a chair leg, for example, set up as if you were routing a short flute, but use a straight bit instead of a round-nose. If the mortise is deeper than ¼ inch, rout it in several passes. (SEE FIGURE 3-11.)

Or, by using a dovetail bit followed by a straight bit, you can rout dovetail slots and flats in a table post. This joint is often used to attach the legs of small pedestal tables and candlesticks. (SEE FIGURE 3-12.)

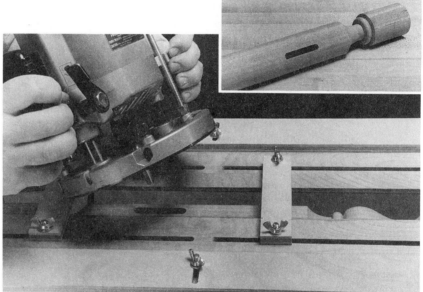

3-11 To cut a mortise in a turned workpiece, mount the workpiece in a fluting jig. Attach stop blocks to the jig's platform to begin and end the cut. Using a straight bit, rout the mortise in the same manner that you might make a reed or a flute. Mortises such as these are often used in ladderback chairs to attach back slats to chair posts. You can also use them to join headboards and footboards to bedposts.

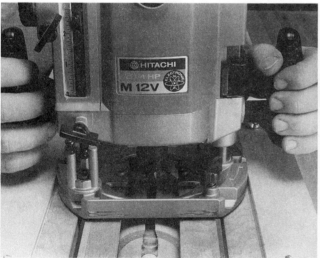

3-12 The legs of pedestal tables are often joined to the posts with sliding dovetail (sometimes called *French dovetail*) joints. To make these joints, rout several dovetail slots in the bottom end of the post with a dovetail bit. Space these slots 120 degrees apart if the table will have three legs, or 90 degrees apart if it will have four. Switch to a straight bit and rout a flat area over each slot — these will accommodate the square shoulders of the dovetail tenons, as shown in the drawing. Finally, mount the same dovetail bit used to make the slots in a table-mounted router and cut the tenons in the legs.

FLUTING JIG

A "fluting jig" holds lathe turnings and other cylindrical workpieces, indexes them, and locks them in place. It also supports and guides a router, enabling you to rout flutes, reeds, and other shapes parallel to the length or axis of the cylinder.

This particular fluting jig holds most small and medium-sized turnings, up to 36 inches long and 4 inches in diameter. It also accommodates all routers with bases from 5⅜ to 7¾ inches in diameter. The indexing wheel has *three* sets of

positioning holes, allowing you to index the turning in increments of 11¼, 15, and 18 degrees. This, in turn, allows you to divide the circumference of the turning in many different ways. In addition, the indexing wheel is *removable* — you can replace it with special indexing wheels designed for specific jobs. **Note:** When drilling indexing holes in the indexing wheel and head plate, use a #29 (.136 inch) drill bit. A 10d nail will fit a #29 hole with almost no slop.

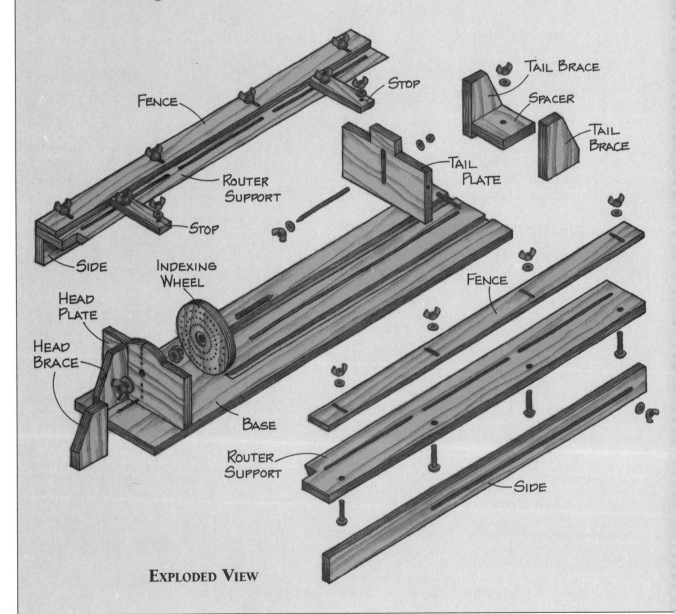

EXPLODED VIEW

1 **To mount a turning in the** fluting jig, adjust the position of the tail assembly so the distance between the indexing wheel and the tailstock is 1 to 2 inches *more* than the length of the turning. Adjust the height of the indexing wheel and "drive" center. There are only two possible positions — the top position is for turnings between 1 and 2½ inches in diameter, and the bottom one is for turnings 2½ to 4 inches in diameter. Place the turning in the jig and seat one end against the drive center. Then advance the "dead" center in the tailstock to seat the other end.

2 **To mount the tail end of the** spindle at a different height than the head, spin a hex nut onto the threaded rod between the head plate and the indexing wheel. This will create some play in the mechanism, allowing you to tilt the spindle.

3 **The dead center can be** raised or lowered to any position from 1 to 3 inches below the platform. This allows you to rout tapered turnings as well as ordinary cylinders. If necessary, raise or lower the dead center so the surface to be routed is parallel to the platform.

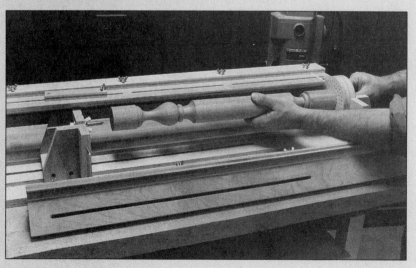

(continued) ▷

FLUTING JIG — CONTINUED

4 **The platform is fitted with** *two* fences, one on either side of the router. This helps to control the router, particularly if you need to do any "back routing." (Back routing is cutting *with* the direction of rotation so that the cutting motion of the bit pulls the router away from the fence or guide.) It also allows you to make cuts that are wider than the bit. For example, if you want to make a $7/16$-inch-wide mortise and only have a $3/8$-inch-diameter bit, set the fences $1/16$ inch farther apart than the diameter of the router base:

$$7/16 - 3/8 = 1/16.$$

There are also two stop blocks to help begin and end the cuts, if you need them.

5 **Once you've mounted the** turning and set the fences and stops, lock the turning so it won't move. Insert the 10d finishing nail through the headstock and into one of the holes in the indexing wheel. Make the first cut, then index the turning before making another — remove the nail, rotate the turning the proper number of degrees, and replace the nail. Make the next cut and index the turning again. Repeat this procedure as necessary.

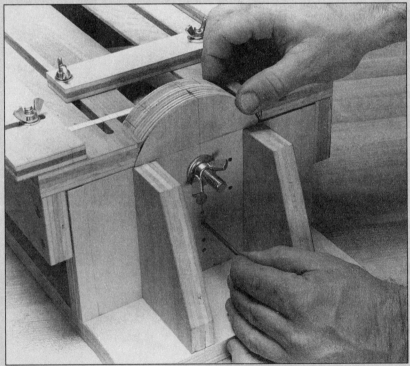

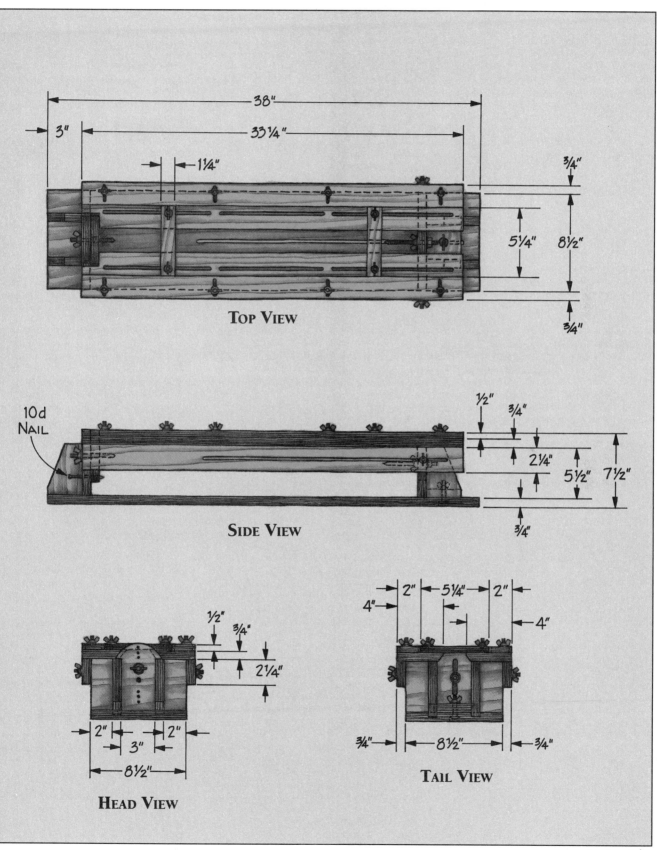

38"

3"

33¼"

1¼"

¾"

5¼"

8½"

¾"

TOP VIEW

10d
NAIL

½"

¾"

2¼"

5½"

7½"

¾"

SIDE VIEW

2"

5¼"

2"

4"

4"

½"

¾"

2¼"

¾"

8½"

¾"

TAIL VIEW

2"

2"

3"

8½"

HEAD VIEW

(continued) ▷

FLUTING JIG — CONTINUED

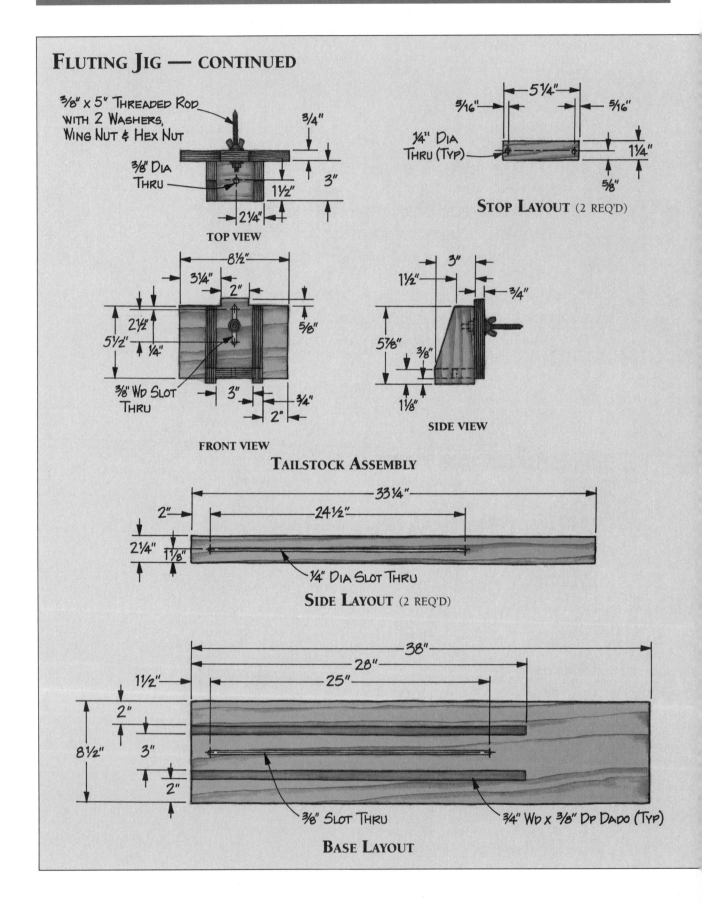

3/8" x 5" THREADED ROD WITH 2 WASHERS, WING NUT & HEX NUT

3/8" DIA THRU

3/4"

3"

1 1/2"

2 1/4"

TOP VIEW

5 1/4"

5/16"

5/16"

1/4" DIA THRU (TYP)

1 1/4"

5/8"

STOP LAYOUT (2 REQ'D)

8 1/2"

3 1/4"

2"

2 1/2"

5 1/2"

1/4"

5/8"

3/8" WD SLOT THRU

3"

3/4"

2"

FRONT VIEW

3"

1 1/2"

3/4"

5 7/8"

3/8"

1 1/8"

SIDE VIEW

TAILSTOCK ASSEMBLY

33 1/4"

24 1/2"

2"

2 1/4"

1 1/8"

1/4" DIA SLOT THRU

SIDE LAYOUT (2 REQ'D)

38"

28"

25"

1 1/2"

2"

3"

8 1/2"

2"

3/8" SLOT THRU

3/4" WD x 3/8" DP DADO (TYP)

BASE LAYOUT

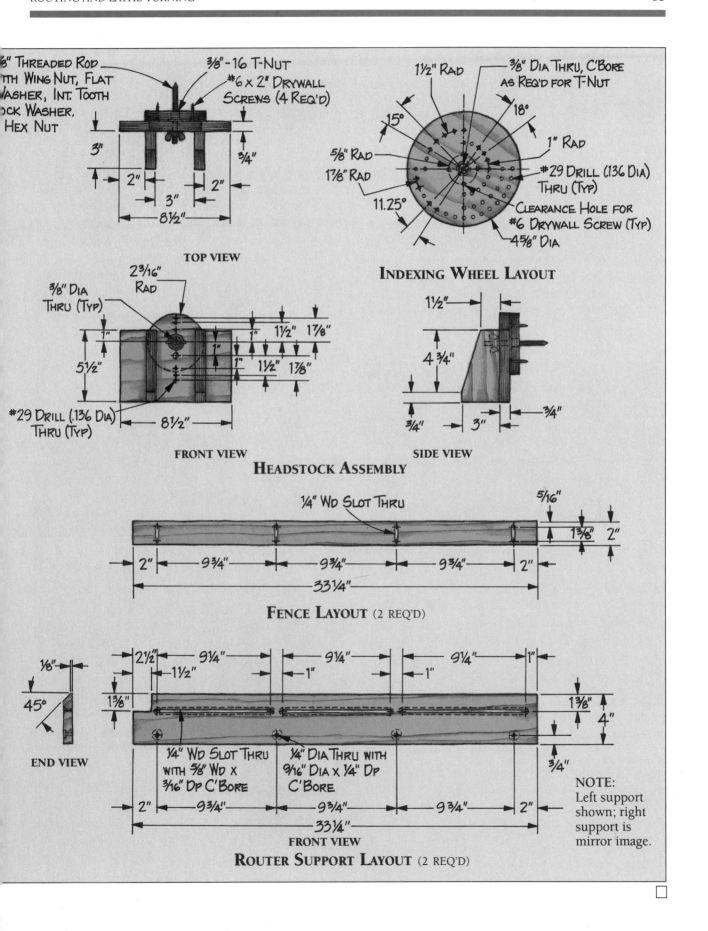

TOP VIEW

INDEXING WHEEL LAYOUT

FRONT VIEW   **SIDE VIEW**

HEADSTOCK ASSEMBLY

FENCE LAYOUT (2 REQ'D)

END VIEW   **FRONT VIEW**

NOTE:
Left support
shown; right
support is
mirror image.

ROUTER SUPPORT LAYOUT (2 REQ'D)

ROUTING PERPENDICULAR TO THE AXIS

To use a router to cut beads, coves, and other shapes *perpendicular* to a lathe turning's axis, the turning must spin as you cut it with a router. For this reason, it's best to mount the turning *and* the router on a lathe. There are two ways to do this. You can erect a routing platform over the turning, attaching legs to the lathe bed, like the fixture shown in FIGURE 3-1. Or, you can attach the router to the lathe tool rest, like the fixture in FIGURE 3-13.

In both setups, you must start each cut with the bit poised close to — but *not* touching — the work, then feed the router into the spinning workpiece *slowly and steadily.* For this reason, it's best to use a plunge router for these operations. Outfit the plunge router with a *Height Adjustor,* as shown on page 40, to feed the bit.

ROUTING BEADS AND COVES

When routing perpendicular to the axis of a turning, you can use almost any *unpiloted* point-cut or top-cut router bit for a wide variety of shapes. For example, a roundover bit produces a bead. Roundnose bits produce small coves, and core-box bits create deeper ones. A straight bit makes a groove or a flat. Ogee bits cut S-shaped curves; V-groove and chamfer bits cut bevels and short tapers. Furthermore, you can combine these shapes to create an almost infinite variety of shapes.

To turn a shape with a router, first mount a workpiece on the lathe and turn it to a cylinder with conventional lathe chisels. Mount the bit you want to use in the router, position the router beside the turning, and adjust the depth of cut so the bit almost touches the turning. (SEE FIGURE 3-14.) Turn both the lathe and the router on, then use the Height Adjustor to slowly feed the bit into the stock. When you reach the desired

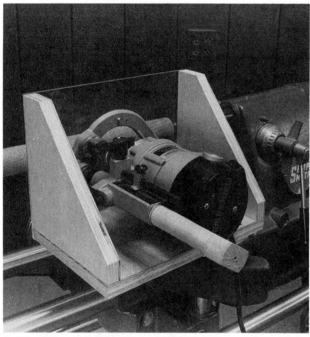

3-13 When you use a router to cut perpendicular to the axis of a turning, you're using it in the same manner as a lathe chisel. So it helps to mount the router in the same place that you use a chisel — on the tool rest. The jig shown actually replaces the tool rest, and mounts the router directly to the tool rest arm. This allows you to use the tool rest mechanisms — arm, post, and carriage — to position the router and lock it in place beside the turning.

3-14 Before routing a shape perpendicular to the axis of a turning, adjust the depth of cut so the router bit is as close to the turning as possible without actually touching it. Before starting the lathe, "swing" the turning (rotate it one full turn by hand) to ensure that it clears the router bit.

depth, back the router out of the cut and turn off both machines. (SEE FIGURE 3-15.)

You'll find that it's extremely time-consuming to turn *all* the shapes on a spindle with a router, simply because you have to constantly change bits. It's much faster to cut them with a lathe chisel. However, this technique can be useful when you want to turn very small shapes, cut duplicate shapes, or make extremely accurate cuts.

DUPLICATING TURNINGS

Some commercial lathe duplicators use small routers to rough out duplicate turnings. In fact, the router duplicator shown in FIGURE 2-18 on page 42 can be used to copy lathe turnings as well as other wooden shapes. However, because these fixtures are expensive and time-consuming to set up, they are only effective when you have large numbers of turnings to duplicate. You can duplicate several turnings much more efficiently (and with less expense) with a router mounted on the lathe tool rest.

To use this setup for duplication, employ an old turner's trick — turn the major and minor diameters of the spindle design first, then fill in the shapes between them. If you can turn the major and minor diameters accurately, the spindles will all match satisfactorily even though the shapes may be slightly different.

First, carefully measure the position and the size of the major and minor diameters on your spindle design. (SEE FIGURE 3-16.) Round the workpieces on the lathe, turning them all to cylinders of roughly the same diameter. Carefully mark the locations of the major and minor diameters on each workpiece. Using a long 1/4-inch-diameter straight bit, rout grooves at each of the marks. Carefully adjust the depth of cut so the diameter of the turning at the bottom of each groove matches the major or minor diameter for that position. When you have routed grooves in all the turnings, remove the router and replace the tool rest. Turn

3-15 Start the lathe and let it come up to speed, then do the same for the router. (Turning on both tools at once may overload a single circuit.) Turn the height adjustor to slowly feed the router into the work. Monitor the depth of cut, either by using a pair of lathe calipers or by watching the depth-of-cut scale on the router. When the cut is the proper depth, stop advancing the router. Back it out of the cut so the bit no longer contacts wood, and turn off both machines.

3-16 To use a router and the router tool rest to duplicate turnings, first measure the shapes in your spindle design. Note the diameters of flat areas, the crests of the beads, and the widest part of the tapers (the major diameters), as well as the bottoms of grooves, the lowest portions of coves, and the narrowest parts of tapers (the minor diameters). Also note the distance of these diameters from the ends of the spindle.

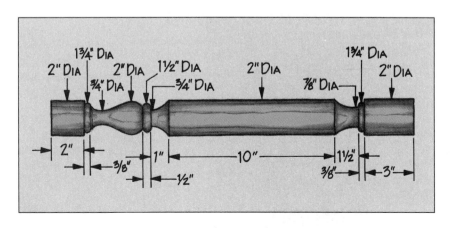

the beads, coves, flats, and tapers with lathe chisels. Stop cutting each shape when you reach the bottom of the corresponding groove. (*SEE FIGURES 3-17 THROUGH 3-20.*)

TRY THIS TRICK

You can also use a router mounted on the lathe to turn round tenons to precise diameters. First, turn the shapes of the workpieces with lathe chisels, cutting the tenons slightly large. Mount the router on the lathe and secure a *large* straight bit in the chuck — the diameter of the bit should match the length of the tenons. Zero the bit with the drive center, mount the turnings on the lathe one at a time, and rout each tenon to the desired diameter.

3-17 Round the workpieces and mark the major and minor diameters of the spindle design on them. Mount a workpiece and the router on the lathe, and install a 1/4-inch-diameter, 3-inch-long straight bit in the router chuck. Lock the arm and post so the router always stays at the *same height* and the *same distance* in relation to the workpiece as you slide the tool rest assembly back and forth. Using the height adjustor, change the depth of cut until the tip of the bit just touches the workpiece. Adjust the pointer on the depth-of-cut stop to "0."

3-18 Back the router bit away from the workpiece, and slide the tool rest assembly to the right or left until the bit is centered over one of the marks for a major or minor diameter. Lock the tool rest assembly in place on the lathe bed and adjust the depth-of-cut stop to halt the router when the bit reaches the desired diameter. Turn on both the lathe and the router, then slowly turn the height adjustor to feed the bit into the turning. Repeat for all the diameters that you have marked on the workpiece.

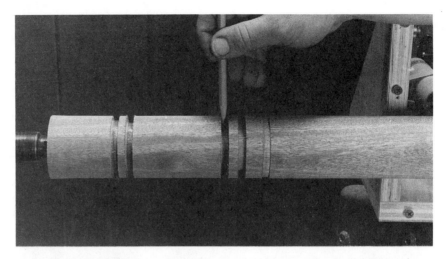

3-19 With the lathe running, mark the bottom of each groove with a pencil. (If the groove is very deep, shave the sides of the pencil so it will reach into the groove.) This will help you gauge the depth of the cuts when you cut the beads, coves, and other shapes in the turnings. If the pencil lines begin to disappear, stop cutting.

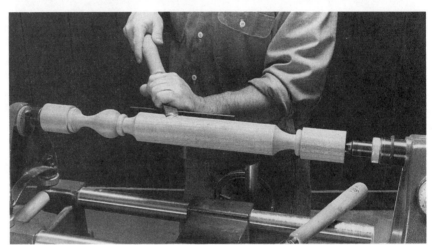

3-20 Remove the router from the lathe and replace the tool rest. Cut the beads, coves, flats, and tapers in the turning with lathe chisels, using the grooves to determine the position and the diameter of each shape. Although the shapes won't be precisely the same from spindle to spindle, the positions and the diameters *will* be, and this makes the turnings appear to be copies of one another. The discrepancies will only be apparent on close inspection, and even then they will seem minor.

MAKING DOWELS

You can use a table-mounted router to turn small dowels with the aid of a "dowel maker." This simple jig works in much the same manner as an old-time rounding plane or *rounder*, cutting square stock into round stock. This allows you to make dowels from any type of wood.

Unlike a rounder, this jig will cut several different sizes of dowels. You can adjust the size of the dowels by changing the plugs in the ends. The infeed plug must have a hole large enough to accommodate the square stock, and the hole in the outfeed plug should be the same size as the dowel you wish to turn.

Here's a list of the stock sizes and plug hole diameters for several common sizes of dowels:

DOWEL SIZE	STOCK SIZE	INFEED HOLE	OUTFEED HOLE
$1/4''$ dia.	$9/32''$ x $9/32''$	$13/32''$ dia.	$1/4''$ dia.
$3/8''$ dia.	$13/32''$ x $13/32''$	$5/8''$ dia.	$3/8''$ dia.
$1/2''$ dia.	$17/32''$ x $17/32''$	$3/4''$ dia.	$1/2''$ dia.
$5/8''$ dia.	$21/32''$ x $21/32''$	$15/16''$ dia.	$5/8''$ dia.
$3/4''$ dia.	$25/32''$ x $25/32''$	$1 1/8''$ dia.	$3/4''$ dia.
$7/8''$ dia.	$29/32''$ x $29/32''$	$1 5/16''$ dia.	$7/8''$ dia.
$1''$ dia.	$1 1/32''$ x $1 1/32''$	$1 1/2''$ dia.	$1''$ dia.

(continued) ▷

MAKING DOWELS — CONTINUED

1 **To use the dowel maker,** mount a ³/₈-inch-diameter straight bit in the table-mounted router. Place the jig over the router so the bit sticks up into the hole in the bottom, and clamp the block to the router table fence. Adjust the depth of cut so the top of the router bit is flush with the bottom edge of the hole.

2 **Check the depth of cut by** routing a small amount of the dowel stock. Turn on the router and feed the stock into the infeed hole, spinning it slowly by hand. If the stock won't feed or is extremely hard to feed, raise the bit slightly. If the dowel that comes out of the outfeed hole is too small, lower the bit.

3 **Slowly spinning the stock by** hand produces a rough cut. To rout a smooth dowel, you must spin the stock much faster. Turn the stock around and secure the short, round "tenon" that you just routed in a hand-held drill. Turn on the router, place the square end of the stock in the infeed hole, and turn on the drill. Slowly feed the stock through the jig while spinning it with the drill.

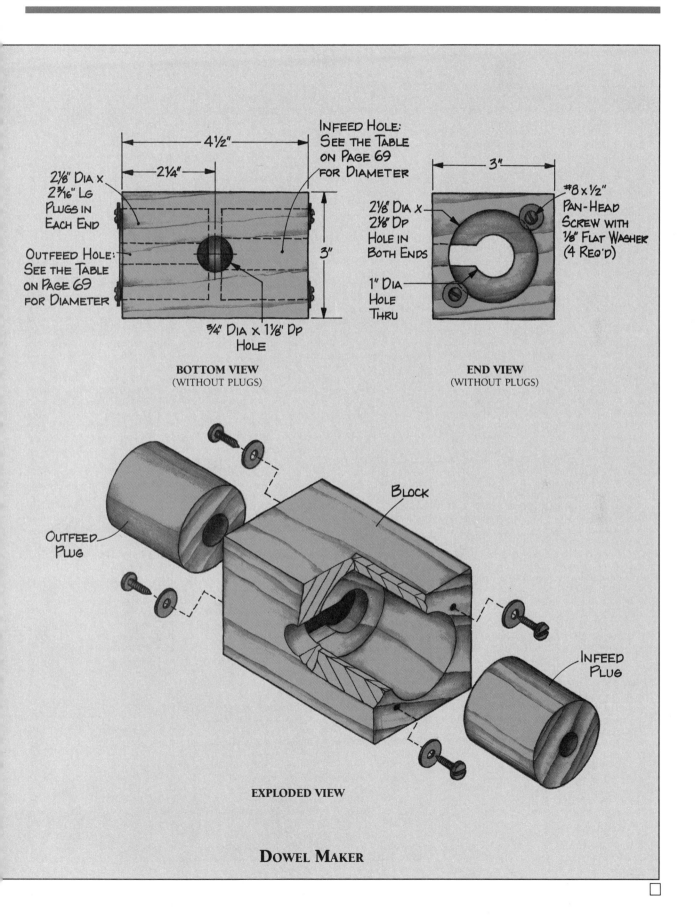

2⅛" DIA x
2³⁄₁₆" LG
PLUGS IN
EACH END

INFEED HOLE:
SEE THE TABLE
ON PAGE 69
FOR DIAMETER

4½"

2¼"

3"

OUTFEED HOLE:
SEE THE TABLE
ON PAGE 69
FOR DIAMETER

¾" DIA x 1⅛" DP
HOLE

BOTTOM VIEW
(WITHOUT PLUGS)

3"

2⅛" DIA x
2⅛" DP
HOLE IN
BOTH ENDS

1" DIA
HOLE
THRU

#8 x ½"
PAN-HEAD
SCREW WITH
⅛" FLAT WASHER
(4 REQ'D)

END VIEW
(WITHOUT PLUGS)

OUTFEED
PLUG

BLOCK

INFEED
PLUG

EXPLODED VIEW

DOWEL MAKER

ROUTER TOOL REST

This simple router mount replaces the tool rest on your lathe, letting you attach a router in its place. A metal post on the underside of the mount fits in the hole in the end of the tool rest arm. This enables you to move the router through the same range of motion as the tool rest — side to side, up and down, in and out — and makes the router a versatile turning tool.

For this setup to work, you need a *plunge router* — this, along with a *Height Adjustor* (see page 40), enables you to feed the router bit into the turning slowly and precisely. Use the smallest plunge router available. You don't need the power of a large router since you can remove only small amounts of stock at a time.

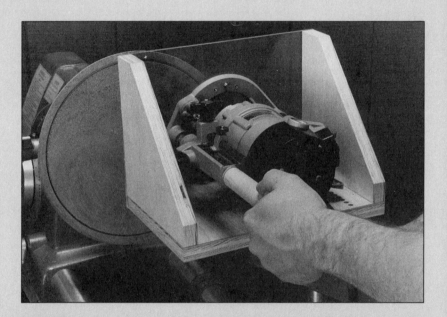

1 **Once the router is mounted** on the tool rest arm, you can place it anywhere that you would ordinarily position the tool rest to hold a lathe chisel. This allows you to use the router for both spindle turning and faceplate turning (shown).

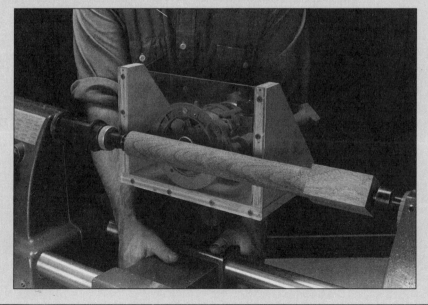

2 **If the design of the lathe** allows you to slide the tool rest carriage from side to side while the tool rest is locked at the same height and the same distance from the turning, you can use this setup to round stock and turn dowels. Set the router the required distance from the turning axis, then slowly draw it along the lathe bed, cutting the workpiece as you go.

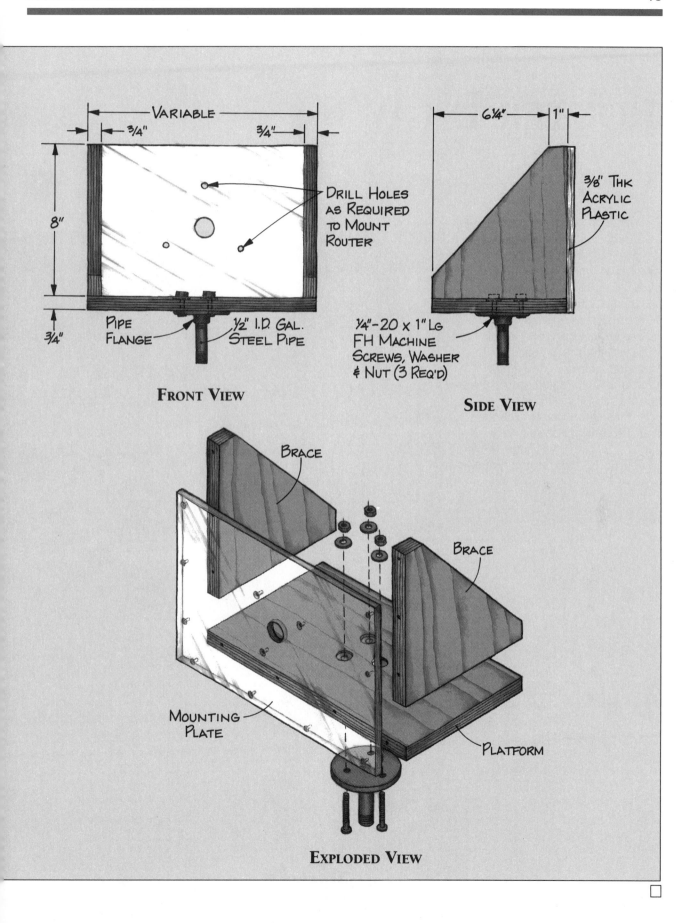

VARIABLE

3/4" 3/4"

DRILL HOLES
AS REQUIRED
TO MOUNT
ROUTER

8"

3/4"

PIPE
FLANGE

1/2" I.D. GAL.
STEEL PIPE

FRONT VIEW

6 1/4" 1"

3/8" THK
ACRYLIC
PLASTIC

1/4"-20 x 1" LG
FH MACHINE
SCREWS, WASHER
& NUT (3 REQ'D)

SIDE VIEW

BRACE

BRACE

MOUNTING
PLATE

PLATFORM

EXPLODED VIEW

4

ROUTER INLAY

You can decorate wooden surfaces by cutting shallow mortises and filling them with inlaid strips of veneer, patches of marquetry and parquetry, slabs of mother-of-pearl, strands of wire, and so on. Because these inlaid objects are often very small and intricately shaped, cutting mortises to fit them requires precision. Not only must the shape be correct, the depth must be accurate and absolutely uniform. One of the best tools for cutting these small, precise mortises is a router.

INLAY TECHNIQUES

INLAYING BANDING

Perhaps the simplest type of decorative inlay is inset wood bandings. These bandings are ribbons of wood that are sliced from a board or a sheet of veneer. They may also be made up of several different contrasting colors of wood, forming long strips of marquetry or parquetry. They are usually straight, but they may also be curved. (SEE FIGURE 4-1.)

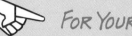

FOR YOUR INFORMATION

The term *marquetry* refers to designs that are made with multiple pieces of wood arranged so the *long grain* shows. *Parquetry* also refers to multiple-piece designs, but the individual pieces are arranged so the *end grain* shows. Marquetry is most often used in furniture; parquetry is more common on floors because the end grain wears much better than the long grain.

To inlay straight banding, first measure its width and thickness. Then rout a shallow rabbet, dado, or groove to fit it, using either a hand-held or a table-mounted router. After cutting the recess, glue the banding in place. (SEE FIGURES 4-2 THROUGH 4-4.)

4-1 Some banding inlays are just thin pieces of wood ripped from boards or cut from sheets of veneer. You can make these simple bandings in your workshop, using a table saw or a veneer knife. Other inlays are intricate pieces of marquetry, made by arranging different colors of wood in geometric patterns, gluing them together, then slicing them into long ribbons. You can make these, too, if you have the patience, but there are many ready-made marquetry bandings available from mail-order woodworking suppliers.

4-2 Cut recesses for banding with the same setups that you might use to cut simple rabbets, dadoes, and grooves. If the workpiece is small, cut it with a table-mounted router using a fence to guide the board. If the workpiece is too large to handle on a router table, use a hand-held router and clamp a straightedge to the workpiece to guide the router. In both cases, use a straight bit to cut the recess.

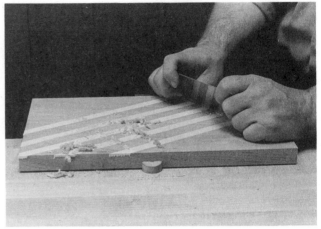

4-3 Test fit the banding in its
recess. When you're satisfied with
the fit, spread glue in the recess and
press the banding in place. Wipe
away any excess glue with a wet rag.
Place a piece of wax paper or plastic
wrap over the banding, then put a
straight, thick board over the covering. Clamp the board to the workpiece. The board helps to distribute
clamping pressure evenly along the
banding while the glue dries. The
wax paper or plastic wrap covering
keeps the board from sticking to the
banding.

4-4 When the glue has dried,
remove the board and the covering.
Carefully scrape away any glue that
remains on the surface. Be careful
not to scrape too deeply — you don't
want to scrape through the banding.
Even if the banding is fairly thick,
you don't want to dish out the surface around it.

FOR BEST RESULTS

When the inlaid materials are fairly thick, rout a
recess that's slightly shallower than the inlay is thick.
This will make the inlay "proud" when you glue it in
place — it will protrude slightly above the surface of
the wood. After the glue dries, scrape or sand the inlay
flush with the surface. But when inlaid materials are
thin, you risk sanding through them if you mount
them proud. Instead, you must rout the recess to
precisely the right depth. Use calipers to measure the
thickness of the inlay, then carefully adjust the router's
depth of cut to match.

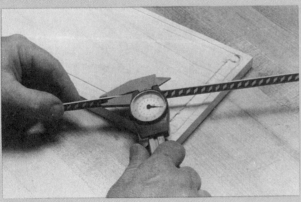

Inlaid banding is not limited to straight lines; you can also inlay curves. For example, several music supply companies offer circular banding to inlay around the sound holes of stringed musical instruments. You can cut recesses for these materials with the router mounted on a single trammel or a circle-cutting jig. Or, you can inlay banding in free-form curves. Cut the banding narrow enough to make it flexible. Using a small router bit and a hand-held router, rout a curved groove. Press the banding into the groove, bending it to fit as you do so. (SEE FIGURES 4-5 AND 4-6.)

4-5 If banding is sufficiently narrow, you can bend it to make a curved inlay. To rout a groove for a curved inlay, either make a template to guide the router or "freehand" the router. For simple designs, you'll get better results if you make a template. For more complex designs (such as the pattern shown), it's easier to cut the grooves freehand.

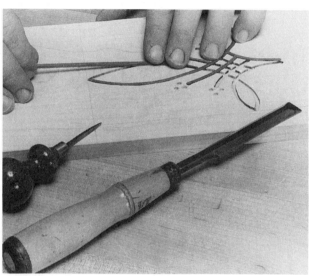

4-6 Spread glue in the routed groove. Starting with one end of the banding, press it into the groove. As you do so, flex the banding to fit the curves of the groove.

TRY THIS TRICK

If the banding is too thick to bend without breaking, you can either make the radii of the curves larger or *heat bend* the banding to fit. To heat bend a banding, mount a short length of pipe so it can be heated by an alcohol lamp. Gently press the banding against the hot pipe, taking care not to get the wood (or your fingers) too close to the flame. In a few moments, the banding will start to "give," bending around the pipe. When you remove the banding and let it cool, the bend will be permanent.

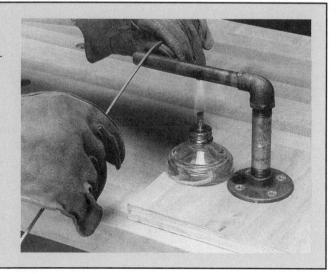

ROUTING MATCHING RECESSES AND INLAYS

In addition to routing recesses for inlays, you can cut wooden inlays with a router. Use a straight bit to do the cutting, and a template and a guide bushing to pilot the router. In fact, if you carefully choose the bit and the bushings, you can rout *both*

the inlay and a matching recess with the *same template!* Use a negative or "cut-out" template (in which the shape to be routed is a hole in the template material), and change the guide bushings for each cut.

1 **When you use a template and** a guide bushing to guide a router, the cutting edge of the bit is offset from the edge of the template by the bushing. When cutting an *outside* shape (such as an inlay) with a cut-out template, this offset is measured from the outside of the bushing to the *farthest* cutting edge. When cutting an *inside* shape (such as a recess), it's measured from the outside of the bushing to the *nearest* cutting edge. If you use a different bushing for each cut and keep the offset the same, the outside shape will match the inside shape (and the inlay will fit the recess). Shown are two combinations of bits and bushings where the offset remains the same for both inside and outside cuts.

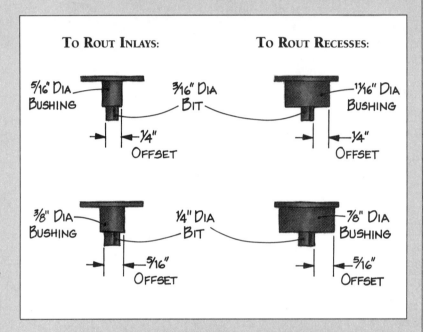

2 **Make a template for the** shape you want to inlay, then rout the inlay from thin wood (at least 1/8 inch thick) with a straight bit and the *smaller* of the two matched guide bushings. **Note:** Keep the shape of the inlay as simple as possible. This procedure becomes more difficult as the inlay shape grows more complex.

3 **Switch to the *larger* of the** two bushings, and rout the recess with the same template and straight bit. Remember, the router bit won't cut sharp *inside* corners. If there are any sharp corners in the inlay design, clean out these areas in the recess with a chisel. Test the fit of the inlay in the recess — it should fit perfectly. When you're satisfied it does, glue it in place.

INLAYING SHAPES

Often, inlay materials are shaped. These shapes can range from simple ovals and diamonds to intricate cutouts and silhouettes. You can cut these shapes from various materials, such as wood, cow's horn, mother-of-pearl, or precious metals; or, you can buy them ready-made. (*SEE FIGURES 4-7 AND 4-8.*)

Note: For the sake of future generations of woodworkers, think twice when choosing inlay materials. Some of the plants and animals that were used extensively in the past are now endangered. For example, the tropical forests that once grew African mahogany, ebony, padauk, and rosewood (both Brazilian and Indian) have been so abused that these species may become extinct. Many botanists advise against purchasing these woods, even from "environmentally responsible" sources. You should also avoid ivory from elephants, walruses, and whales for the same reason. Instead, substitute tagua nuts (vegetable ivory) or hog tusks.

4-7 There are many shaped inlays available from commercial sources, manufactured for various types of woodworking projects. For example, you can purchase marquetry "patches" in several shapes and designs for classical furniture reproductions. Luthiers (makers of stringed musical instruments) often inlay fingerboards and pegboards with slices of mother-of-pearl and abalone, cut to resemble diamonds, flowers, and leaves.

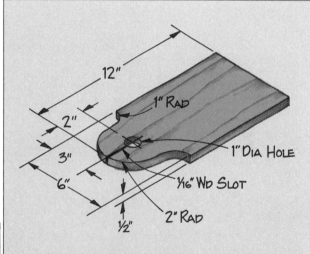

4-8 You can also make your own shapes from thin sheets of wood, metal, and many other materials. Cut these materials on a scroll saw, provided the shapes are large enough to handle safely. To cut small shapes, use a jeweler's saw, supporting the materials with a shopmade saw table, as shown. Work slowly, using a very light pressure on the blade.

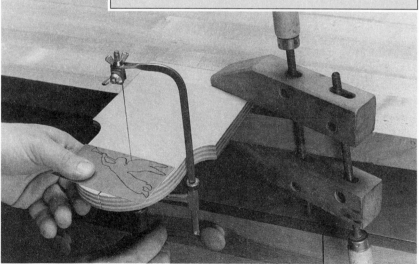

WHERE TO FIND IT

You can purchase ready-made veneer marquetry patches from:

The Woodworkers' Store
4365 Willow Drive
Medina, MN 55340

Constantine's
2050 Eastchester Rd.
Bronx, NY 10461

To buy uncut slabs of mother-of-pearl and precut pearl inlay shapes, write:

Stewart-MacDonald Manufacturing Co.
Box 900
Athens, OH 45701

Tagua nuts (vegetable ivory) are available from:

Lee Valley
1080 Morrison Dr.
Ottawa, Ontario K2H 8K7

Garrett Wade
161 Avenue of the Americas
New York, NY 10013

Hog tusks can be purchased from most hobby stores and rock shops — businesses that sell lapidary materials. You can buy thin sheets of pewter, silver, and other precious metals from jewelers' suppliers. Sheets of copper and brass are available from dealers who specialize in those materials — look in the Yellow Pages under "Copper" or "Brass."

Finally, if you want to use exotic woods, particularly species that grow in rain forests, you can obtain a free list of suppliers who get their wood from environmentally friendly loggers and sawyers by writing:

The Rainforest Alliance
270 Lafayette St.
State Route 512
New York, NY 10012

Woodworkers Alliance for Rainforest Protection
Box 133
Coos Bay, OR 97420

The Rainforest Alliance also provides a list of endangered woods — species that should not be purchased from *any* source.

To inlay shaped materials, you must rout a shaped recess to fit them. Place the shape on the surface where you want to inlay it, then trace around it with a pencil, scratch awl, or knife. Remove the shape and rout out *most* of the waste from the recess, stopping the bit just short of the line. Remove the rest of the waste with hand tools — carving chisels, "dogleg" chisels, and a small router plane. Fit the shape to the recess, then glue it in place. (SEE FIGURES 4-9 THROUGH 4-13.)

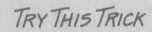

TRY THIS TRICK

If you install several inlays that are all the same shape, make a template to help cut the recesses. Attach a guide collar to the router to follow the template.

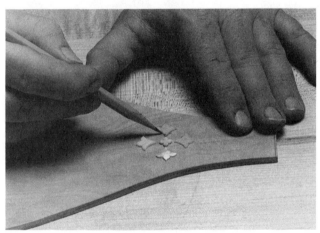

4-9 To inlay a shape, you must first trace the outline on the wood surface. This is sometimes a difficult task, particularly if the design includes several small shapes. To keep *wooden* shapes from shifting as you trace around them, stick them to the surface with double-sided carpet tape. To keep *hard, dense materials* such as mother-of-pearl or metals in place, glue them to the wood surface with white (polyvinyl resin) glue. The adhesive won't hold the inlays in place permanently, but it will secure them long enough to trace their outline. Afterwards, you can easily remove them from the surface by placing a block of softwood against the inlay edges and striking the block sharply with a mallet.

4-10 Rout the inlay recesses with a straight bit and a hand-held router. You'll find it's easier to work with small bits rather than large ones — not only can you cut intricate details with small bits, but they are also easier to control. You may wish to work with a small router rather than a large one — small routers give you better visibility and are easier to control. However, even with a small bit and a small router, you may find it difficult to rout a line freehand. For this reason, stop cutting just short of the outline.

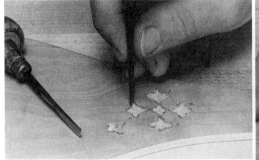

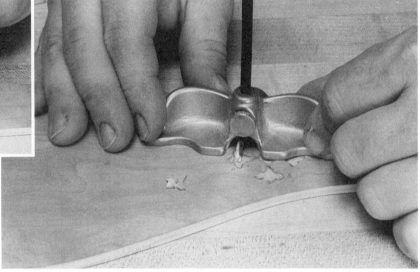

4-11 Trim up to the line with carving chisels. Use gouges to cut the curved portions of the shape, and a skew chisel to cut straight edges and corners. Then clean out the waste with dogleg chisels and a small router plane.

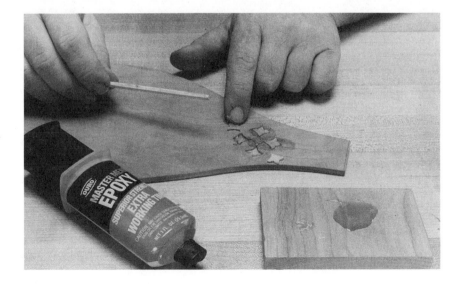

4-12 Test fit the inlays in the recesses. If they won't fit, or if the fit seems extremely tight, trim away a little more stock from the edges of the recesses with hand tools. When the inlays fit properly, glue them in place. Use yellow (aliphatic resin) glue to secure wood and veneer inlays, and epoxy glue for metal, mother-of-pearl, and other hard, dense materials.

4-13 Let the glue dry completely,
then scrape away the excess. If the
inlay is proud, *hand* sand it flush
with the surrounding surface. *Don't*
use a power sander, because inlays
tend to be very thin and you might
sand right through them. Also, many
exotic woods produce toxic sawdust,
and you don't want to kick this sawdust into the air with a power sander.
Finally, power sanding generates a
great deal more heat from friction
than hand sanding. If you're sanding
metal inlays, this heat may cause
them to expand, break the glue bonds,
and pop out of their recesses. If
you're sanding mother-of-pearl, the
heat will release a toxic gas.

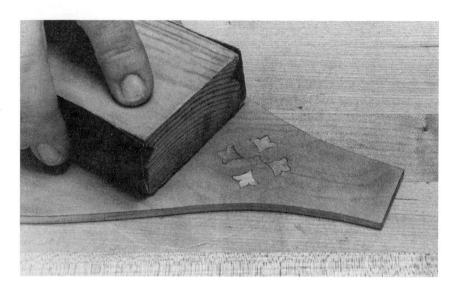

4-14 Eighteenth- and early-
nineteenth-century country craftsmen simulated classical ivory inlays
with sulphur. They cut decorative
mortises and grooves, heated sulphur powder until it liquified, then
poured the molten sulphur into the
recesses. After the sulphur cooled,
they sanded it flush with the wood
surface. The result was a cream-
colored inlay that looked a good deal
like ivory. *Photo courtesy Winterthur
Museum.*

INLAYING WIRE AND SULPHUR

In addition to cutting mortises to fit rigid materials,
you can also manipulate *malleable* materials to fit the
mortises. For example, some old-time craftsmen cut
decorative mortises, then filled them with molten
sulphur. When the sulphur cooled, it formed hard,
cream-colored inlays that mimicked ivory. Other
craftsmen routed long, narrow grooves, then bent
wire to follow the contours of these grooves. (*SEE
FIGURES 4-14 AND 4-15.*)

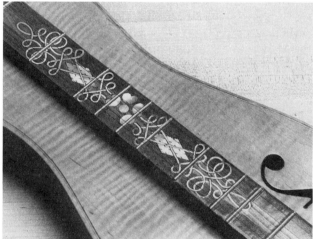

4-15 This wire inlay decorates
the fretboard of an Appalachian dul-
cimore. It's made from dozens of
pieces of silver wire, each bent and
cut to fit routed grooves. The mother-
of-pearl diamonds were added after
the wire was installed.

Traditional sulphur inlaying is a moderately dangerous task. As you heat the sulphur, it releases noxious fumes. If you get it too hot, it may start to burn. And when you pour it, you must protect yourself against possible spills and splashes. However, you can reproduce the *appearance* of sulphur inlay with clear epoxy cement. Mix the epoxy resin with powdered pigments to create an ivory color, add the hardener, then spread the cement in routed recesses, and let it cure. (*SEE FIGURES 4-16 AND 4-17.*)

To inlay metal wire, first rout narrow grooves for the wire. The width of the grooves must be the same diameter as the wire, and the depth must be slightly less. Bend the wire to fit the grooves and cut it to length. Fill the grooves with epoxy cement and press the wire into the grooves. After the epoxy has cured, hand sand the wire flush with the surrounding surface using aluminum oxide and silicon carbide sandpaper. (*SEE FIGURES 4-18 THROUGH 4-20.*) **Note:** You can purchase wire made from precious metals from most jewelers' suppliers.

> ## TRY THIS TRICK
>
> **Y**ou can also use cream-colored stick shellac to fill routed recesses and imitate old-time sulphur inlay.

4-16 Sulphur inlay was devised in the eighteenth century as an inexpensive substitute for ivory. Today, there are other materials that will achieve the same visual effect and that are safer and simpler to use. Perhaps the simplest is epoxy cement. First, rout decorative grooves or mortises for the inlay. Mix epoxy resin with white and yellow powdered pigments to make a cream-colored paste, then add the hardener. Spread the cement in the recesses and let it cure.

4-17 After the epoxy has hardened completely, sand it flush with the surrounding surface. In addition to simplicity and safety, this material has another advantage over the old-time sulphur inlay that it imitates: It is far more durable — cured epoxy is not as brittle as cooled sulphur, and it adheres more tenaciously to the wood.

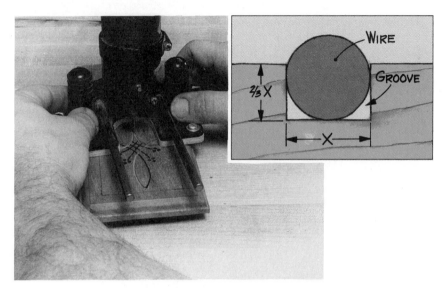

4-18 To inlay wire, lay out the inlay design on the wood surface. Rout narrow grooves with a straight bit and a hand-held router, carefully following the design. The width of the grooves should be the same as the diameter of the wire, and the depth should be about two-thirds of the diameter.

4-19 Bend pieces of wire to fit the grooves and cut them to length. Cut each piece a little long and grind the ends flat; otherwise, the installed wire inlay will look "pinched" at the ends. Where the end of one wire butts against the side of another, grind a "miter" so there are no gaps between the two wires. When you have cut all the wire pieces, test fit them in the grooves. Remove the wire, fill the grooves with epoxy cement, and press the wire back into the grooves.

4-20 Let the epoxy cure at least 24 hours (even if it's the quick-cure variety), then *hand* sand the inlay. This will remove the excess epoxy, create a flat surface along the wire, and grind that surface flush with the wood. Use progressively finer sandpaper, starting with 120-grit aluminum oxide and working up to 600-grit silicon carbide to polish the metal surface.

Projects

5

TIP-AND-TURN TABLE

A small pedestal table with a top that tipped and turned was an interesting eighteenth-century innovation. It was used as a serving table during formal dinners and teas. The rotating top operated like a lazy Susan, making it easy to reach all the dishes on the table. When dinner was over and the table was no longer needed, the top was tilted to the vertical position and the table was stored against a wall.

Originally, most of the joinery and shaping required to make these tables was done by hand, but today you can reproduce many portions of this classic design with the aid of a router. On the table shown, the lipped oval top was created with a router and a double trammel jig. The decorative reeds in the post were cut with a router and a fluting jig. The fluting jig was also used to cut the dovetail mortises and tenons that join the legs to the post.

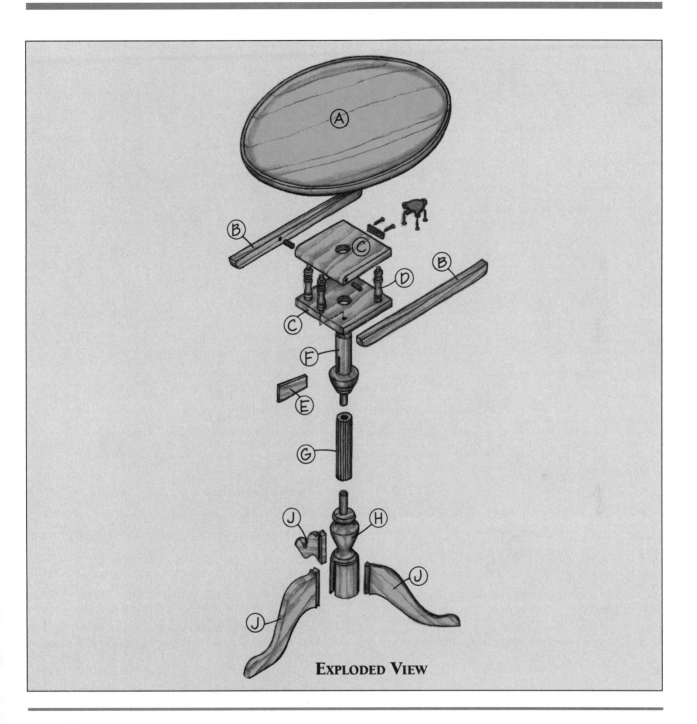

EXPLODED VIEW

MATERIALS LIST (FINISHED DIMENSIONS)

Parts

A.	Top	7/8" x 18" x 24"
B.	Braces (2)	3/4" x 1 1/4" x 17 3/4"
C.	Birdcage top/ bottom (2)	3/4" x 6 3/4" x 6 3/4"
D.	Spindles (4)	7/8" dia. x 4"
E.	Key	1/4" x 2" x 4"

F.	Top post	2 7/8" dia. x 8"
G.	Middle post	1 3/4" dia. x 8 3/8"
H.	Bottom post	2 7/8" dia. x 10 3/4"
J.	Legs (3)	3/4" x 4" x 12 3/4"

Hardware

#8 x 1 1/2" Flathead wood screws
(8)

3/8" diameter x 1" Steel pins (2)

Table top catch and mounting
screws

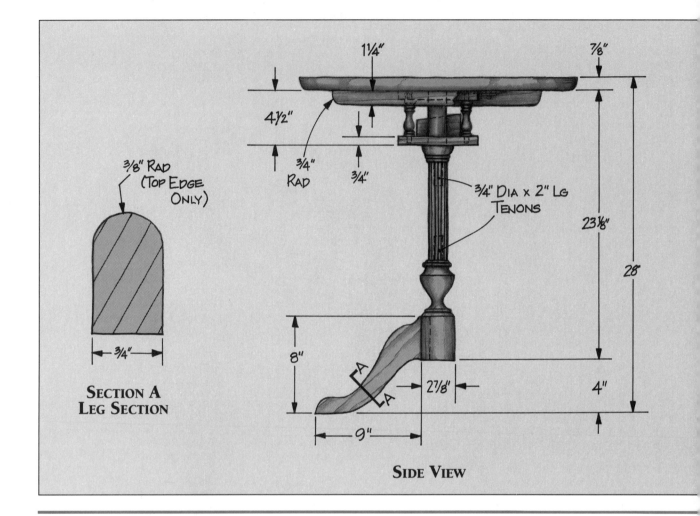

3/8" RAD (TOP EDGE ONLY)

**SECTION A
LEG SECTION**

3/4"

1 1/4"

7/8"

4 1/2"

3/4" RAD

3/4"

3/4" DIA x 2" LG TENONS

23 1/8"

28"

8"

2 7/8"

4"

9"

A A

SIDE VIEW

PLAN OF PROCEDURE

1 Select the stock and cut the parts to size.
To make this table, you need a 12/4 (twelve-quarters) turning blank about 30 inches long, and about 7 board feet of 4/4 (four-quarters) lumber. You can use almost any cabinet-grade hardwood, although classic American furniture is typically made from mahogany, walnut, cherry, or maple. The tip-and-turn table shown is made from "blistered" maple, a rare form of figured maple.

Cut the turning blank into three sections to make the top, middle, and bottom posts. Each section should be 3 inches square and 1 or 2 inches longer than specified in the Materials List. From the rough 4/4 lumber, cut four smaller turning blanks, each 1 inch square and about 5 inches long. These will become the spindles. Plane the remaining 4/4 wood to 7/8 inch thick and glue up stock to make a wide board at least 19 inches wide and 25 inches long —

this will become the top. Plane the remaining stock to 3/4 inch thick and cut the leg blanks, braces, birdcage top, and birdcage bottom to size. Finally, resaw or plane a small piece of 3/4-inch-thick stock to 1/4 inch thick and cut the key.

2 Cut the oval top. Lay out the major and minor axes of the oval shape on the top board. The major axis (which runs through the length of the oval) should be 24 inches long, and the minor axis (which is perpendicular to the major axis) should be 18 inches long. Draw these axes so they bisect each other in the middle of the stock.

Using double-faced carpet tape, mount a double trammel jig where the axes cross. (For instructions and plans on how to make a *Trammel Jig,* see page 45.) Mount a 1/4-inch straight bit in a router and attach the router to the jig's beam. Attach the beam to the pivots;

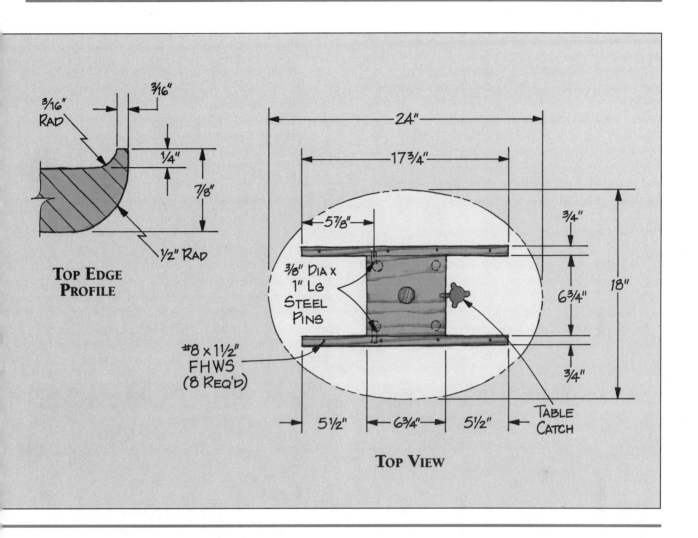

TOP EDGE PROFILE

3/16" RAD

3/16"

1/4"

7/8"

1/2" RAD

24"

17 3/4"

5 7/8"

3/8" DIA X 1" LG STEEL PINS

#8 x 1 1/2" FHWS (8 REQ'D)

3/4"

6 3/4"

18"

3/4"

TABLE CATCH

5 1/2"   6 3/4"   5 1/2"

TOP VIEW

the major pivot should be 9 inches away from the router bit's *inside* cutting edge (the edge nearest the pivot), and the minor pivot 12 inches away. Turn on the router and carefully swing the beam around the pivots, cutting an oval 18 inches wide and 24 inches long. (*SEE FIGURE 5-1.*)

5-1 Rout the oval shape of the top with a ¼-inch straight bit, swinging the router around a double trammel jig. (This device guides the router in an elliptical path.) Make several complete turns around the pivots, cutting ⅛ to ¼ inch deeper with each turn until you cut completely through the stock.

3   Rout the lip in the top.   Detach the beam from the major and minor pivots, but do *not* detach the jig from the top. Remove the straight bit from the router and replace it with a ³⁄₈-inch core-box or roundnose bit. Mount the beam on the pivots with both pivots ¹⁄₂ inch closer to the bit than when you cut the outside edge. Adjust the depth of cut to ¹⁄₄ inch.

Hold the router slightly above the stock. (The beam will flex slightly, allowing you to do this.) Turn it on and gently lower it into the wood. Swing it around the pivots, cutting a ³⁄₈-inch-wide, ¹⁄₄-inch-deep groove. The *outside* edge of the groove should be ³⁄₁₆ inch away from the top's edge. (*See Figure 5-2.*)

4   Rout the recess in the top.   The top is scooped out like a very shallow bowl. Although the top is ⁷⁄₈ inch thick at the edge, the interior is just ⁵⁄₈ inch thick, as shown in the *Top Edge Profile*.

You can scoop out this recess with a router. Mount a wide straight bit in the router, then mount the router to an oversize sole or a long platform. The platform from the *Overhead Routing Jig* (see page 119) serves nicely, or you can make a platform from a scrap of plywood. Adjust the depth of cut to ¹⁄₄ inch and rest the platform on the top lip. Move the router and the platform back and forth, routing out the waste from the interior of the top. As you do so, be careful not to cut into the lip. (*See Figure 5-3.*)

5   Cut the shapes of the legs and braces.   Stack the leg blanks face to face, securing them to each other with double-faced carpet tape. Enlarge the *Leg Pattern* and trace it onto the top blank. Using a band saw or saber saw, cut the shapes of all three legs at once. Sand the sawed edges with a disk sander and a drum sander, then take the legs apart and discard the tape.

Stack the braces face to face and tape them together. Lay out the ³⁄₄-inch radii on the bottom corners, cut the round corners, and sand away the saw marks.

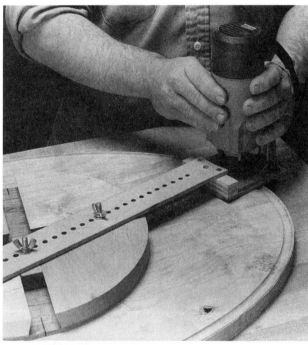

5-2   Replace the straight bit with a ³⁄₈-inch core-box bit, then shorten the "swing" of the beam (the distance between the pivots and the bit) by ¹⁄₂ inch. Be sure to keep the same spacing between the major and minor pivots. Then cut a ¹⁄₄-inch-deep, round-bottom groove just inside the edge of the top. This will form a lip around the perimeter of the oval.

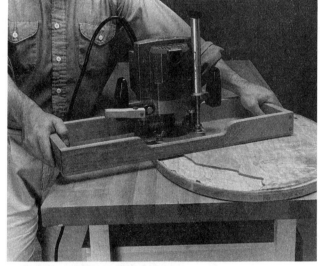

5-3   Use a wide straight bit (³⁄₄ to 1 inch in diameter) to create the recess in the top. With the router mounted on a long platform, "plane" the interior of the top so it's thinner than the lip. Work from the lip in toward the center, always keeping *both* ends of the platform resting on high spots — either the lip or a portion of the waste that hasn't yet been routed away. **Note:** The platform should be at least 20 inches long. Otherwise, you won't be able to rout out the waste in the very center of the top.

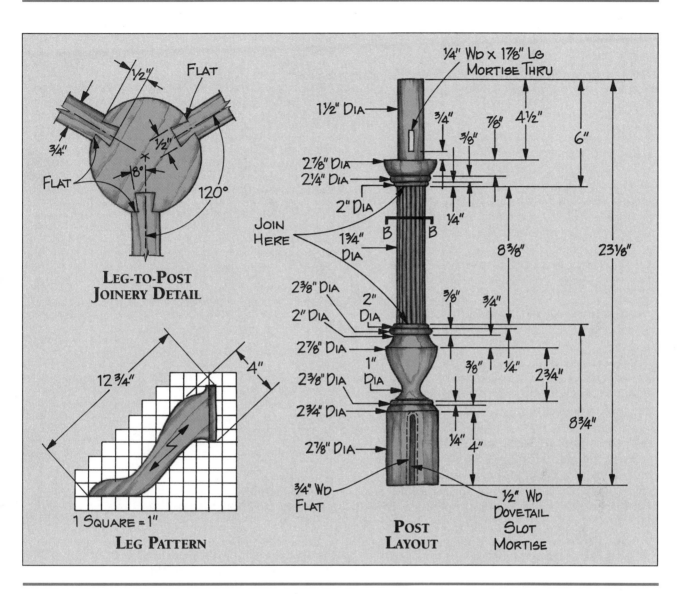

LEG-TO-POST JOINERY DETAIL

LEG PATTERN

1 Square = 1"

POST LAYOUT

6 Cut the mortises in the top post and birdcage top. The tenon on the top end of the top post serves as a pivot for the birdcage — the mechanism that allows the table to turn. The birdcage is held in place with a key that fits through a mortise in the tenon. It's easier to cut this mortise *before* you turn the stock, while it's still square.

Carefully lay out the location of the shapes and the tenons that you will turn. Also lay out the 1/4-inch-wide, 1 7/8-inch-long mortise, as shown in the *Post Layout*. Drill a series of overlapping 1/4-inch-diameter holes to remove most of the waste from the mortise, then clean up the edges and the corners with a chisel.

Using chisels, cut a mortise in the edge of the birdcage top for the catch plate. This mortise must be the same size and shape as the plate. Around the perim-

eter, it should be as deep as the plate is thick; near the center, it should be deep enough to accept the catch.

7 Rout the dovetail tenons and slots. Round the bottom post, making a cylinder 2 7/8 inches in diameter. Do *not* turn the beads and coves yet. Mount the cylinder in a fluting jig and rout three 1/2-inch-wide, 1/2-inch-deep, 4-inch-long blind dovetail slots in the bottom end, as shown in the *Post Layout*. These slots must be spaced evenly around the circumference, every 120 degrees, as shown in the *Leg-to-Post Joinery Detail*. Also rout 3/4-inch-wide, 4-inch-long flats over the slots. Square the ends of the flat areas with a chisel. (See "Routing Along the Length of a Turning" on page 53 for further details.)

Using the same dovetail bit you employed to rout the dovetail slots, cut ½-inch-wide, ½-inch-long tenons in the upper ends of the legs. (SEE FIGURE 5-4.) Round the top edge of each tenon with a rasp or a file to fit the blind ends of the slots.

8   Turn the posts and spindles.   Turn the top, middle, and bottom posts to the shapes shown in the *Post Layout.* Also turn four identical spindles, as shown in the *Spindle Layout.* Note that the top and bottom posts each have ¾-inch-diameter, 2-inch-long tenons on *one* end. These tenons join the parts to the middle post. The spindles also have tenons on *both* ends to attach them to the top and bottom of the birdcage. After turning the shapes, finish sand each piece on the lathe.

9   Rout the reeds in the middle post.   Mount the middle post on the fluting jig. Using a point-cut ⅛-inch roundover bit, rout 16 ¼-inch-wide reeds around the post's circumference. Index the post 22½ degrees between each cut, as shown in the *Middle Post Section.* For more information, see "Routing Along the Length of a Turning" on page 53.

10   Drill holes in the braces, middle post, birdcage top, and birdcage bottom.   Lay out the holes in the faces and edges of the birdcage top and bottom, as shown in the *Birdcage Top/Bottom Layout.* Also, mark the locations of the pivot pin holes in the braces and the tenon holes in the ends of the middle post. Then drill these holes:

■ a 1½-inch-diameter hole through the center of the birdcage top and bottom

■ ⅜-inch-diameter, ½-inch-deep holes in the *inside* faces of the birdcage top and bottom to attach the spindles

■ ⅜-inch-diameter, ½-inch-deep holes in the edges of the birdcage top and the *inside* faces of the braces to hold the pivot pins

■ ¾-inch-diameter, 2-inch-deep holes in both ends of the middle post

11   Round the edges of the table top, birdcage top, and legs.   Using a router and a roundover bit, rout a radius in these edges:

■ Cut a ½-inch radius in the bottom edge of the table top, as shown in the *Top Edge Profile.*

■ Cut a ⅜-inch radius in the top edge of the birdcage top, near the pivot pin hole, as shown in the *Side View* of the *Birdcage Top/Bottom Layout.* This edge must be rounded for the top to tilt.

■ Cut a ⅜-inch radius in the top edge of the legs, as shown in the *Leg Section.*

12   Taper and fit the key.   Cut the taper in the key, as shown in the *Key Layout,* then fit the key to the mortise in the top post. The key must fit snugly, and when it's inserted into the mortise as far as it will go, it should protrude an equal distance from *both* sides.

13   Assemble the table.   Finish sand all the *flat* parts that you've made so far. (The turned parts have already been sanded on the lathe.) Glue the top, middle, and bottom posts together, then glue the legs to the post assembly. Also, glue the spindles to the birdcage top and bottom. Let the glue dry.

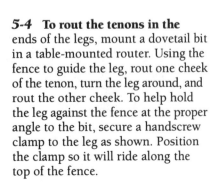

5-4   To rout the tenons in the ends of the legs, mount a dovetail bit in a table-mounted router. Using the fence to guide the leg, rout one cheek of the tenon, turn the leg around, and rout the other cheek. To help hold the leg against the fence at the proper angle to the bit, secure a handscrew clamp to the leg as shown. Position the clamp so it will ride along the top of the fence.

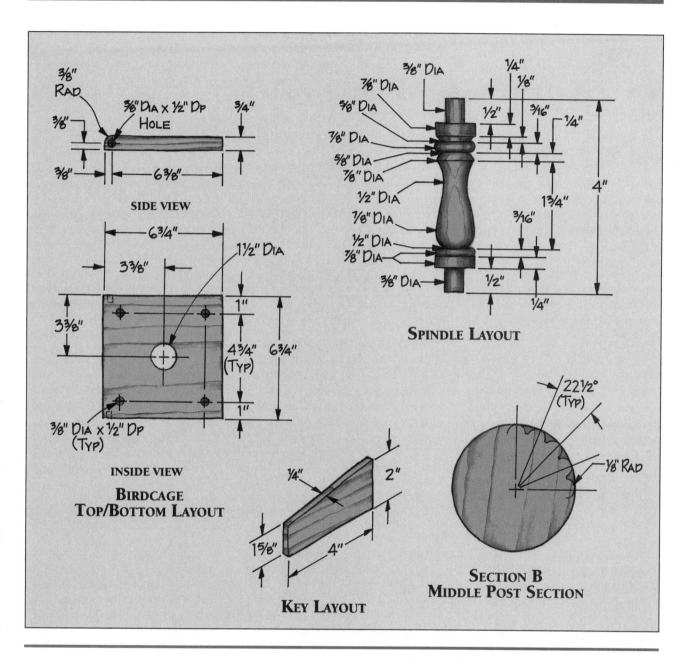

SIDE VIEW

INSIDE VIEW
BIRDCAGE TOP/BOTTOM LAYOUT

SPINDLE LAYOUT

KEY LAYOUT

SECTION B MIDDLE POST SECTION

Screw the catch plate in its mortise in the birdcage top. Turn the birdcage assembly and the table top upside down on the workbench. Center the birdcage on the top and insert the steel pivot pins in their holes. Place the braces next to the birdcage, fitting the pins in the holes in the brace. Screw (but *don't* glue) the braces to the top with flathead screws, countersinking the screw heads. Also, attach the catch to the table top.

Turn the top assembly right side up and place it over the tenon on the top of the post. Insert the key in the mortise and *lightly* tap it in place with a mallet. Make sure that the top tips and turns easily.

14 Finish the table. When you have assembled all the parts and you're satisfied that the table top tips and turns properly, disassemble the table. Remove the key from its mortise and take the top assembly off the post. Remove the braces, screws, pins, catch, and catch plate from the top assembly. Set the hardware and fasteners aside.

Do any necessary touch-up sanding, then apply a finish to all wooden surfaces. The table shown was stained to look like antique maple, then finished with several coats of orange shellac. When the finish dries, reassemble the table.

6

Snowflake Bench and Table

Asimple shape often becomes more appealing when you *repeat* it. The bench and table shown here prove this point — the engaging "snowflake" patterns are made up of simple shapes, repeated over and over. The boards that form the bench back and the table top are all cut to precisely the same shape. Each board is a wedge — a portion of a circle. When arranged side by side, these shaped wedges form an intricate circular (or semi-circular) design.

There are many ways to cut the shapes in the boards, but one of the easiest is to *pattern rout* each piece. Once you've made a template to guide the router, you won't have to lay out the shaped wedges or worry about following the cut lines. You can rout as many wedges as you need, and each wedge will be shaped precisely the same.

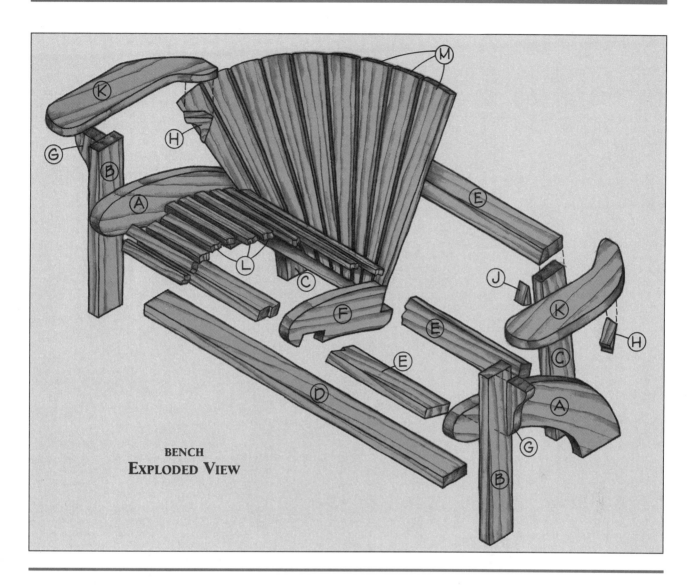

BENCH
EXPLODED VIEW

MATERIALS LIST (FINISHED DIMENSIONS)

Parts

Bench

A. Back
    legs (2)   1½" x 9¼" x 28¾"

B. Front
    legs (2)   1½" x 3½" x 21½"

C. Back
    braces (2)   1½" x 3½" x 20¾"

D. Long
    stretcher   1½" x 3½" x 45"

E. Short
    stretchers (3)   1½" x 3½" x 42"

F. Seat brace   1½" x 6¾" x 18"

G. Front arm
    braces (2)   1½" x 3" x 7"

H. Back arm
    braces (2)   1½" x 3¼" x 3¼"

J. Back spacers (2) 1" x 1½" x 3"

K. Arms (2)   1" x 8" x 19"

L. Seat
    slats (10)   ¾" x 1½" x 48"*

M. Back
    slats (17)   ¾" x 3½" x 28"*

*For simplicity, cut all these parts to the
lengths specified. After fitting, some will
be cut shorter.*

Hardware

Bench

#10 x 2½" Brass flathead wood
  screws (42–48)

6d Galvanized finishing nails
  (¼ lb.)

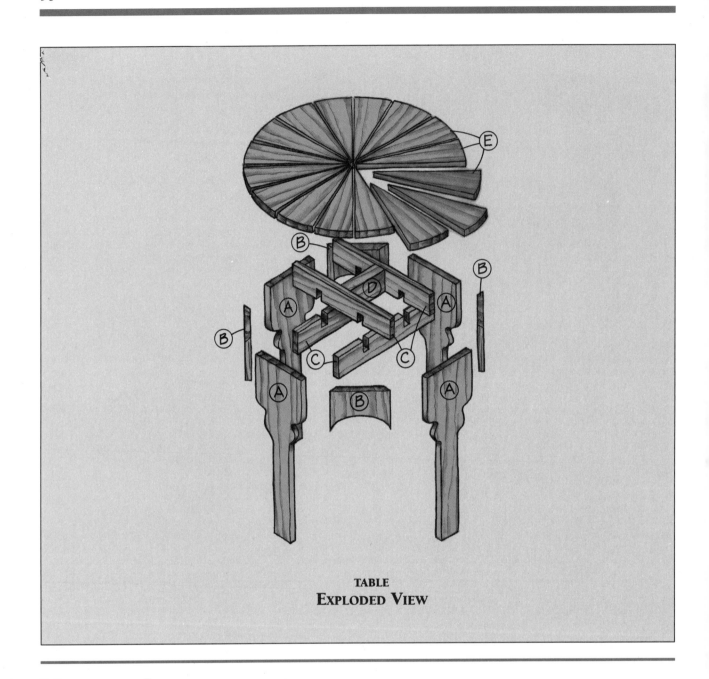

TABLE
EXPLODED VIEW

MATERIALS LIST (FINISHED DIMENSIONS)

Parts

Table

A. Legs (4) $\frac{3}{4}$" x 7" x 21$\frac{1}{4}$"
B. Aprons (4) $\frac{3}{4}$" x 6$\frac{23}{64}$" x 4$\frac{1}{2}$"
C. Cross
   braces (4) $\frac{3}{4}$" x 2$\frac{1}{2}$" x 14$\frac{1}{2}$"
D. Center
   brace   1$\frac{1}{2}$" x 2$\frac{1}{2}$" x 5$\frac{1}{2}$"
E. Top
   slats (16) $\frac{3}{4}$" x 3$\frac{3}{4}$" x 10$\frac{7}{8}$"

Hardware

Table

#10 x 1$\frac{1}{2}$" Brass flathead wood
   screws (30–36)
6d Galvanized finishing nails
   ($\frac{1}{4}$ lb.)

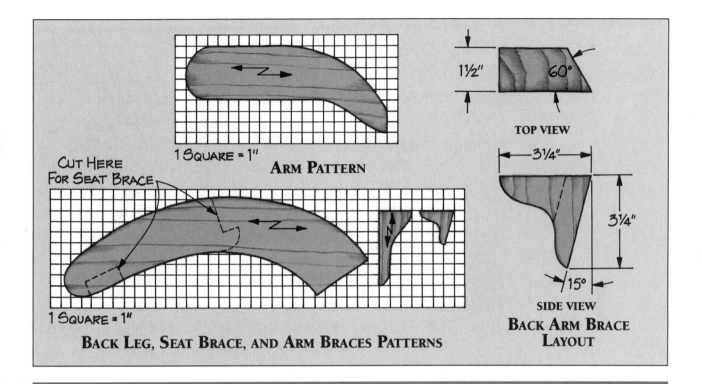

1 SQUARE = 1"   **ARM PATTERN**

CUT HERE
FOR SEAT BRACE

1 SQUARE = 1"

BACK LEG, SEAT BRACE, AND ARM BRACES PATTERNS

1½"   60°

TOP VIEW

3¼"

3¼"

15°

SIDE VIEW
BACK ARM BRACE LAYOUT

PLAN OF PROCEDURE

1 Select the lumber. To make the snowflake bench, you need approximately 25 board feet of 8/4 (eight-quarters) stock, 4 board feet of 5/4 (five-quarters) stock, and 22 board feet of 4/4 (four-quarters) stock. The table requires an additional 12 board feet of 4/4 stock and a scrap of 8/4 stock. If you plan to use this project outside, you should use a rot-resistant, cabinet-grade wood such as redwood, cypress, cedar, or juniper. If you plan to paint the project and keep it in a semi-protected area, such as a covered porch, you can use an inexpensive utility wood such as pine or poplar. The bench and table shown were made from pine, then finished with exterior paint.

Note: Do not use pressure-treated lumber or other construction-grade wood. These materials are not seasoned as carefully as cabinet-grade woods, and they may warp, bow, or split after you build the bench and table.

MAKING THE BENCH

2 Cut the parts to size. Plane the 8/4 stock to 1½ inches thick and cut the legs, braces, and stretchers to the sizes shown in the Materials List. Bevel the edges of the two short stretchers to which the back slats are attached, as shown in the *End View*. Also bevel the

back edges of the back arm braces, as shown in the *Back Arm Brace Layout*. Miter the bottom ends of the back braces.

Plane the 5/4 stock to 1 inch thick and cut the arms. Also plane the 4/4 stock to ³/₄ inch thick, then cut all the slats.

3 Cut the shapes of the legs, braces, and spacers. Enlarge the patterns for the back legs, seat brace, arms, and arm braces, as shown in the *Back Leg, Seat Brace, and Arm Braces Patterns* and the *Arm Pattern*. Trace these patterns onto the stock. Also lay out the spacers, as shown in the *End View*. Cut the shapes of these parts with a band saw or saber saw. Sand the sawed edges.

TRY THIS TRICK

To save work, *pad saw* and *pad sand* identical parts. For example, stack the stock for the back legs face to face, securing the boards with double-faced carpet tape. Saw and sand both legs at once, then take the boards apart and discard the tape. You can do the same for the arms, arm braces, and spacers.

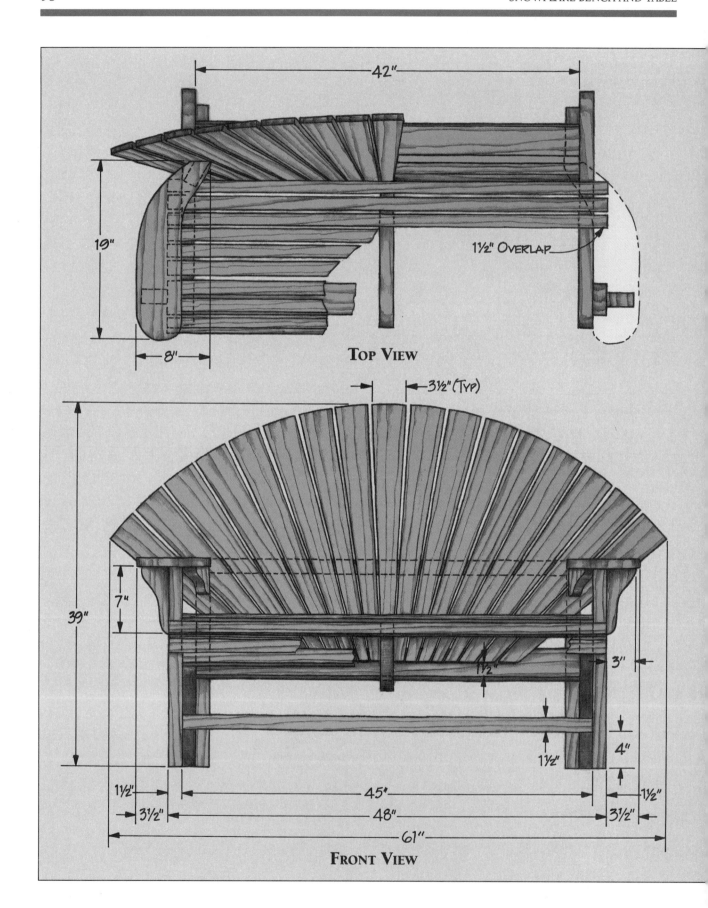

42"

19"

8"

1½" OVERLAP

TOP VIEW

3½" (TYP)

39"

7"

1½"

3"

4"

1½"

1½"

1½"

3½"

3½"

45"

48"

61"

FRONT VIEW

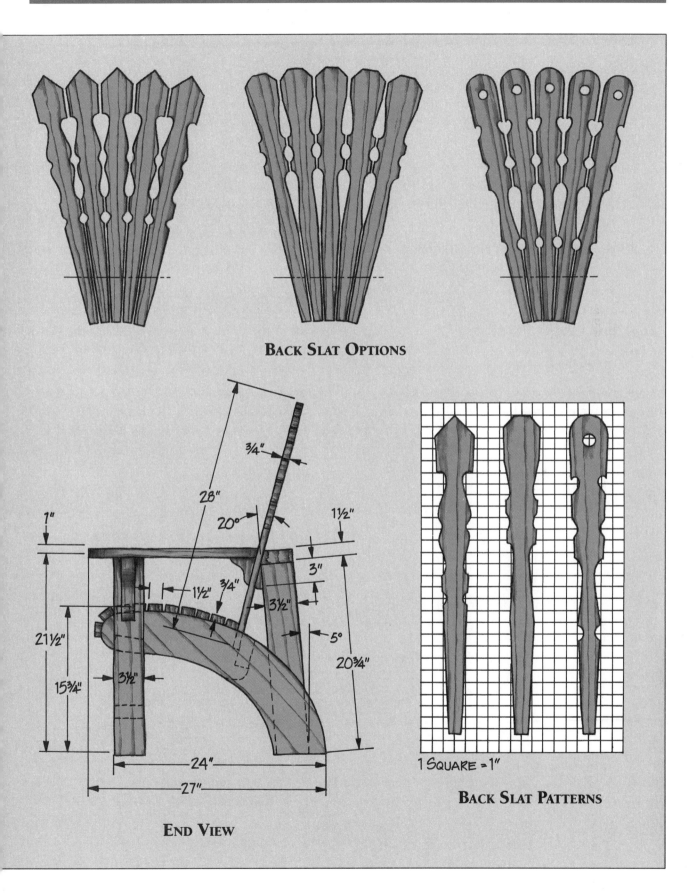

BACK SLAT OPTIONS

END VIEW

BACK SLAT PATTERNS

1 SQUARE = 1"

4 Rout the shapes of the back slats. When you need to make only one or two copies of a part (such as the legs, braces, or spacers), it's easier to cut them on a band saw. However, there are 17 identical back slats. When you have this many identical parts to turn out, it saves effort to make a template and rout them.

First, decide on a pattern for the back slats. There are three possibilities shown in the *Back Slat Options* and *Back Slat Patterns,* or you can design your own. Enlarge the pattern and trace it onto one of the slat blanks. Cut out the shape with a band saw and sand the sawed edges. This first slat will serve as a template for the remaining 16.

Attach the completed slat to another blank. Rout the shape in the second board, using either a pattern-cutting bit or a pin routing setup. Repeat for all the remaining blanks. Refer to "Pattern Routing" on page 28 for detailed instructions on how to use a pattern-cutting bit or setup for pin routing.

5 Assemble the frame. Lightly sand all the parts to smooth any rough surfaces. If you wish, slightly round the edges of the parts to help prevent splinters. Then make three separate frame subassemblies. First, assemble one of the beveled short stretchers to the back braces with flathead wood screws. Second, join the back legs, seat brace, and the remaining short stretchers. Third, attach the front legs to the long stretcher.

Temporarily clamp these three subassemblies together to make the frame. Check that the beveled edge of the short stretcher on the back brace subassembly is aligned with the face of the beveled stretcher on the back leg subassembly. If these two surfaces are misaligned, loosen the clamps and move the back brace subassembly forward or back. Both surfaces must be in line so the back slats will rest flat against them.

When the subassemblies are all properly positioned, screw them together. Countersink the heads of all the screws flush with or slightly below the surface.

6 Attach the back slats. Tack the back slats to the beveled stretchers with finishing nails — but *don't* hammer the nails all the way in. Start with the middle slat, then work toward the right and the left, spacing the slats evenly. Remember to put the spacers under the slats that cover the top ends of the back braces. When you're satisfied with the arrangement of the slats on the frame, mark a straight line horizontally across the bottom ends of the slats. This line should be about 1½ inches up from bottom edge of the lower stretcher, as shown in the *Front View.* Remove the slats one at a time, trim the bottom ends across the line you just marked, then reassemble the slats to the frame. When all the slats have been trimmed, drive the nails home. Set the nail heads slightly below the wood surface.

7 Attach the seat slats. Tack the seat slats to the back legs and seat brace with finishing nails. Once again, *don't* drive the nails all the way in. Start with the back seat slat and work toward the front, spacing the slats evenly. Trim the ends of the slats as needed to fit them between the front legs. When all the seat slats are in place and you're satisfied with the arrangement, drive the nails home and set the heads.

8 Attach the arms. Join the front arm braces to the front legs and the back arm braces to the back slats with flathead wood screws. Then screw the arms to the braces and the top ends of the front legs. Countersink the heads of the screws.

9 Finish the bench. If you wish, fill the voids over the nail heads and screw heads with *epoxy* putty. (Other wood fillers may not stand up to the weather.) Do any necessary touch-up sanding to the wood surfaces, then apply an exterior finish. The bench shown is finished with exterior latex paint.

MAKING THE TABLE

10 Cut the parts to size. Plane the 4/4 stock to ³/₄ inch thick and cut the legs, cross braces, and slats to the sizes given in the Materials List. Rip the aprons to the width listed, but cut them about ½ to 1 inch longer than specified. Plane the 8/4 stock to 1½ inches thick and cut it to size.

11 Cut and assemble the brace work. Lay out the notches in the cross braces as shown in the *Cross Brace Layout.* Cut these out with a band saw or a saber saw. Assemble the cross braces *without* fasteners to test the fit of the lap joints. When you're satisfied that they fit properly, reassemble them with finishing nails. Also, nail the center brace in place.

12 Fit the legs and aprons. Temporarily tack the legs to the ends of the cross braces, but *don't* drive the nails all the way in. Miter the ends of the aprons at 45 degrees, fitting them between the legs. However, *don't* attach them yet. When the aprons are fitted, remove the legs from the brace work.

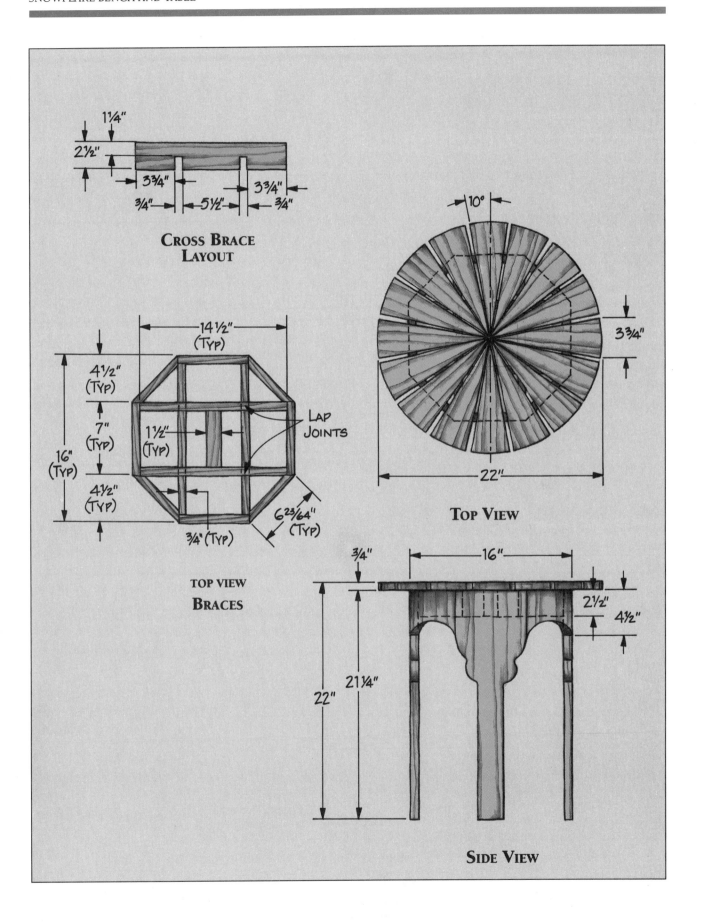

CROSS BRACE LAYOUT

1¼"

2½"

3¾"

3¾"

¾"

5½"

¾"

14½" (TYP)

4½" (TYP)

7" (TYP)

1½" (TYP)

16" (TYP)

4½" (TYP)

LAP JOINTS

6²³⁄₆₄" (TYP)

¾" (TYP)

TOP VIEW BRACES

10°

3¾"

22"

TOP VIEW

¾"

16"

2½"

4½"

21¼"

22"

SIDE VIEW

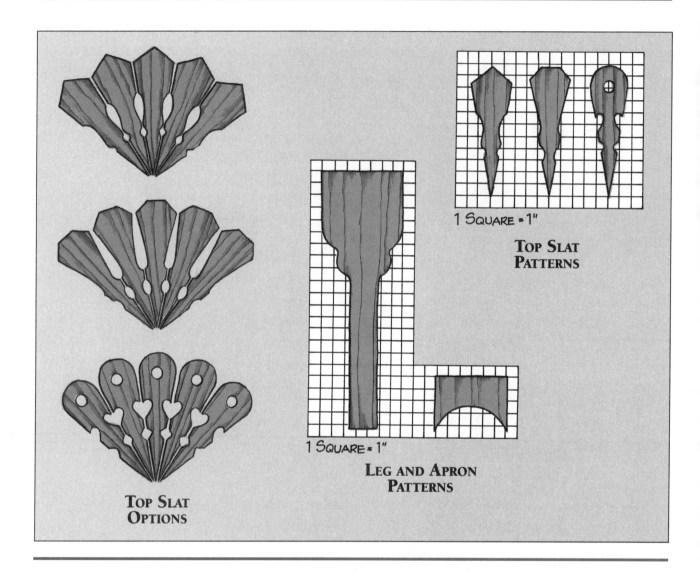

**TOP SLAT
OPTIONS**

1 SQUARE = 1"

**LEG AND APRON
PATTERNS**

1 SQUARE = 1"

**TOP SLAT
PATTERNS**

13 **Cut the shapes of the legs and aprons.**
Enlarge the *Leg and Apron Patterns* and trace them
onto the stock. Cut the shapes of these parts with a
band saw or saber saw and sand the sawed edges. To
save work, *pad saw* and *pad sand* these parts.

14 **Rout the shapes of the top slats.** Choose a
pattern for the slats that matches the bench. There are
three possibilities shown in the *Top Slat Options* and
Top Slat Patterns, or you can design your own. Enlarge
the pattern and trace it onto one of the slat blanks.
Cut out the shape with a band saw and sand the
sawed edges. This will serve as a template for the
remaining 15 slats.

Attach the completed slat to another blank. Rout the
shape in the second board, using one of the pattern
routing techniques described in *Step 4* on page 100.

15 **Attach the legs, aprons, and slats.** Attach
the legs to the ends of the cross braces with flathead
wood screws. (Drive these screws through the nail
holes.) Then attach the aprons to the edges of the legs.
Countersink the heads of the screws.

Arrange the top slats to form a circle on top of the
brace work, spacing the boards evenly as shown in the
Top View. Tack the slats to the brace work with finishing nails, but *don't* drive the nails all the way in until
you have tacked down all the slats and you're satisfied with the arrangement. Set the heads of the nails.

16 **Finish the table.** If you wish, fill the voids
over the heads of the nails and screws. Do any necessary touch-up sanding to the wood surfaces, then
apply an exterior finish to match the bench.

7

ROUTER WORKBENCH

There are many different fixtures that will hold a router so it can be used as a stationary tool. Three of the most useful are a router table, a router arm, and a joint maker. Each of these accessories holds a router so it can be used as a stationary tool. And each increases the versatility of the router in a different way, depending on how it holds the router in relation to the work. A router table holds the router beneath a work surface, so you can pass the work over it. A router arm suspends the router above the work, and a joint maker holds it to one side.

This *router workbench* does the job of all three tools. With the router fastened vertically beneath the work surface of the bench, you can use it as a router table; workpieces can be guided past the cutter either freehand or with the help of a fence or miter gauge. Mount the router vertically in the *overhead routing jig,* and you can perform many of the same tasks that you would ordinarily do on a router arm, such as pin-routing duplicate shapes and performing other overhead routing tasks. With the router mounted horizontally in the *mortise-and-tenon jig,* the workbench becomes a joint maker; you can make a variety of woodworking joints, including perfectly matched mortises and tenons.

Although this may seem like an imposing project, it can be easily

built at your own pace. The bench is *modular,* so you can break the project up into several simple steps. There are three modules — the workbench itself, the overhead routing jig, and the mortise-and-

tenon jig. Choose the modules you want and build them as you have the time. The router workbench shown was built one piece at a time over several months by Dane and Doug Crowell.

103

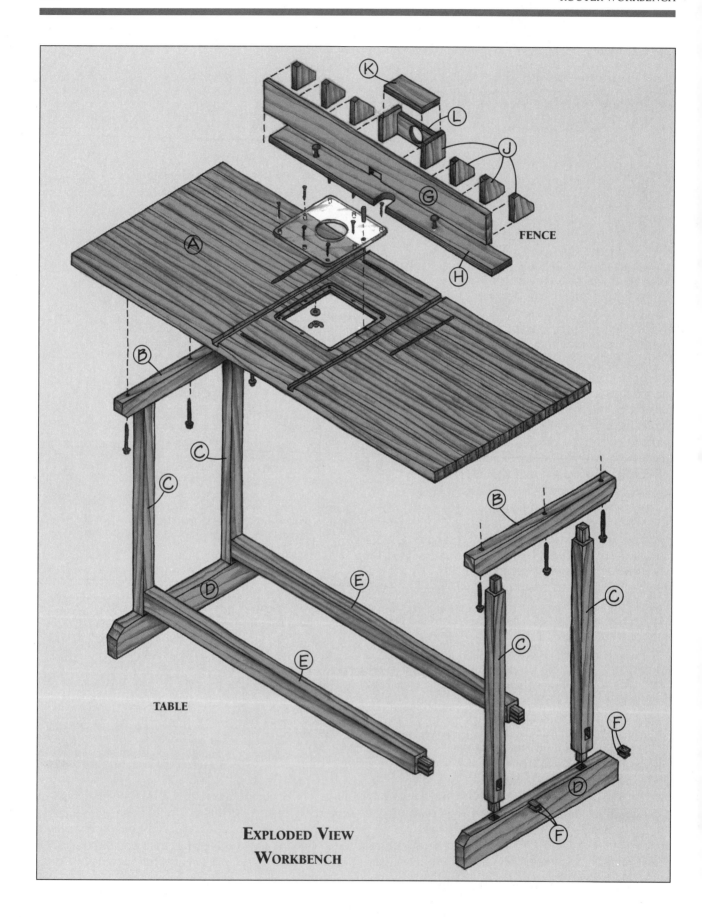

FENCE

TABLE

EXPLODED VIEW
WORKBENCH

ROUTER WORKBENCH

MATERIALS LIST (FINISHED DIMENSIONS)

Parts

A. Table top   1½" x 25" x (variable)

B. Top braces (2)   1¾" x 2½" x 23"

C. Legs (4)   1¾" x 1¾" x 32"

D. Feet (2)   1¾" x 3½" x 25"

E. Stretchers (2)   1¾" x 2½" x (variable)

F. Wedges (8)   ³/₃₂" x 1" x 1½"

G. Fence face   ¾" x 4" x 36"

H. Fence base   ¾" x 3¼" x 36"

J. Fence braces (8)   ¾" x 3¼" x 3¼"

K. Dust collector top   ¾" x 3¼" x 6"

L. Dust collector back   ¾" x 2½" x 6"

Hardware

³/₈" x 3½" Lag screws (6)

³/₈" Flat washers (6)

³/₈" Transparent acrylic plastic sheet (size variable)

#8 x 1" Flathead wood screws (8)

Miter gauge (from table saw or band saw)

⅝" lg. Flathead machine screws (3) to fit router base

¼" x 2" Steel pin

#8 x 1¼" Flathead wood screws (42–48)

³/₈" x 3" Carriage bolts (2)

³/₈" Flat washers (2)

³/₈" Wing nuts (2)

Combination switch/outlet (optional)

Metal switch box (optional)

Outlet plate (optional)

Cable clamp/box connector (optional)

14/3 Electrical appliance cord (10'-optional)

Grounded plug (optional)

PLAN OF PROCEDURE

1 Decide the size of the table. As shown in the drawings, the router table is 60 inches long. Although you might first think that you don't have room for a large table, it can actually *save* space by doubling as your workbench. If you want to make a smaller router table, however, simply shorten the table to fit the available space. When you have decided on how big to make the table top, calculate the length of the stretchers.

2 Cut the parts. Decide what material you will use to make the top. The top shown is a maple "butcherblock" countertop. Many lumberyards and building supply stores carry these countertops in standard sizes — 25 x 48 inches, 25 x 60 inches, and so on. (If these businesses don't have them on hand, they may be willing to place a special order for you.) You can also make your own wooden slab, or make the top from plywood or medium-density fiberboard. After selecting the material, cut the top to size.

Cut the top braces, legs, feet, stretchers, wedges, and fence face from a hard, durable wood such as oak or maple. Make the remaining parts from plywood.

3 Cut the shapes of the feet, top braces, and fence braces. One or more corners of the feet, the top braces, and six of the fence braces are "relieved."

These corners are cut at 45 degrees, as shown in the *Workbench/Side View* and *Fence/End View*. Make these cuts on a table saw or band saw. Sand the sawed edges.

4 Cut the shapes of the fence face and base. The fence face and base are notched to fit around the router bits, as shown in the *Fence/Front View* and *Fence/Top View*. Lay out these notches and cut them with a band saw or saber saw. Sand the sawed edges.

5 Drill holes in the workbench top braces, dust collector back, and fence base. Using a hole saw or fly cutter, cut a 2¼-inch-diameter hole through the dust collector back, as shown in the *Fence/End View*. This will enable you to hook a standard 2½-inch-diameter vacuum hose to the completed collector. (The standard hose connectors taper down to 2¼ inches.)

Drill three ⁷/₁₆-inch-diameter holes through the edge of each top brace, as shown in the *Workbench/Side View*. The locations of these holes are not critical, but they should be spaced evenly along the length of each top brace. Later, you'll use these holes to attach the table top to the braces.

Also drill two ³/₈-inch-diameter holes through the fence base, as shown in the *Fence/Top View*. Unlike the holes in the top braces, the locations of these holes *are* critical. They must be precisely 19¾ inches apart.

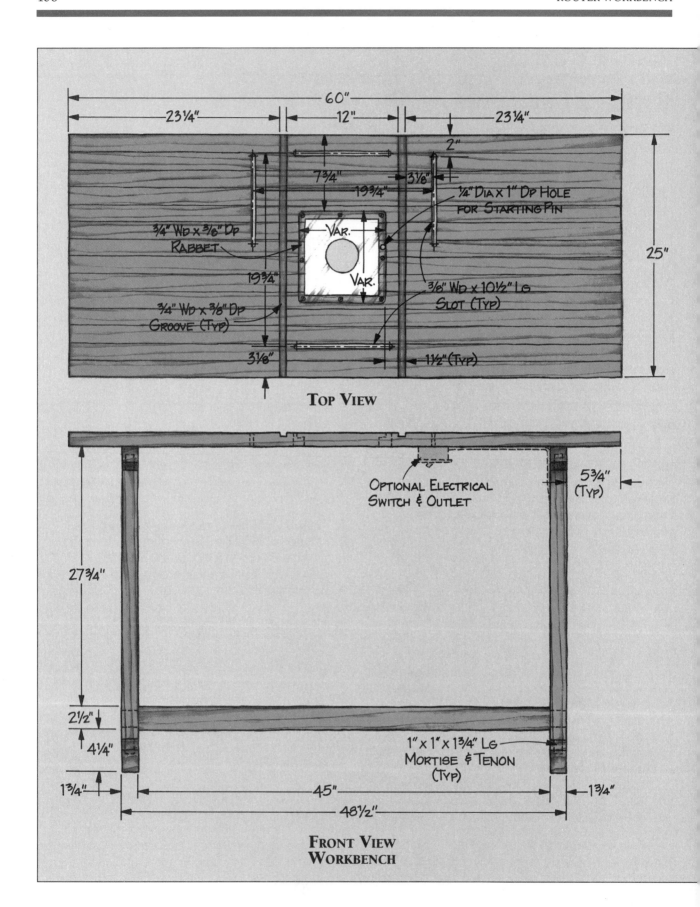

TOP VIEW

FRONT VIEW
WORKBENCH

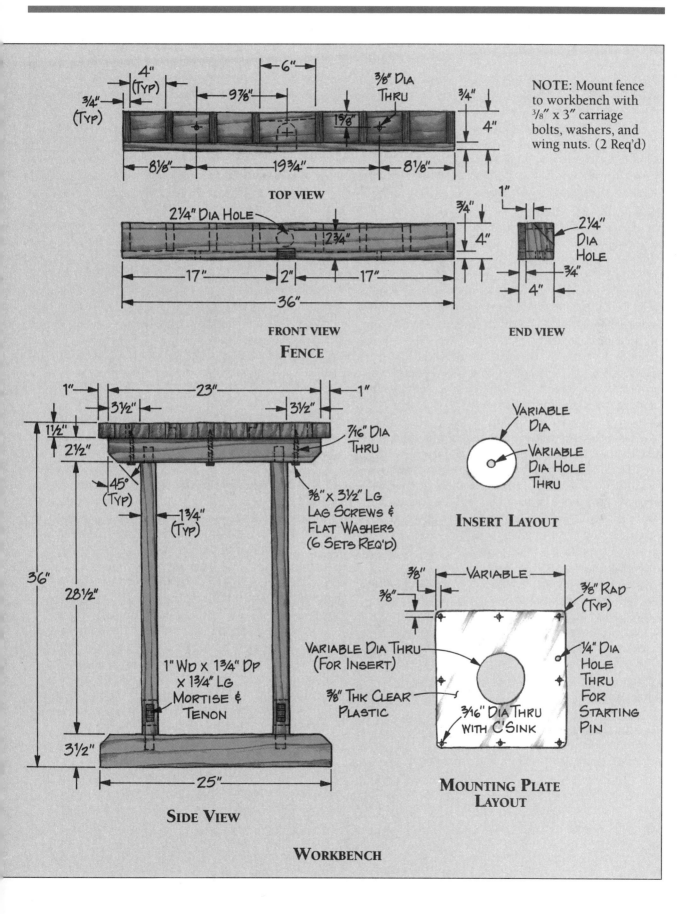

TOP VIEW

FRONT VIEW

END VIEW

NOTE: Mount fence to workbench with 3/8" x 3" carriage bolts, washers, and wing nuts. (2 Req'd)

FENCE

SIDE VIEW

INSERT LAYOUT

MOUNTING PLATE LAYOUT

WORKBENCH

6   Cut the mortises and tenons.   The workbench frame — top braces, legs, feet, and stretchers — is assembled with mortises and tenons. Make the mortises first, then fit the tenons to them.

Using a table saw or band saw, cut two $1/16$-inch-wide, $1\,3/4$-inch-deep kerfs in each stretcher tenon, as shown in the *Workbench/Side View* and the *Workbench/Joinery Detail*. Also, cut 1-inch-wide, $1\,1/4$-inch-long wedges to fit the kerfs. These wedges should taper from $3/32$ inch thick at one end to a knife edge at the other.

7   Assemble the router workbench.   Dry assemble the top braces, legs, feet, and stretchers to check the fit of the mortise-and-tenon joints. Disassemble the parts and sand them smooth, then reassemble them with glue. Tap the wedges into kerfs in the ends of the stretcher tenons. When the glue dries, cut the wedges even with the ends of the tenons. Sand all the joints clean and flush.

Center the table top on the frame and secure it with $3/8$ x $3\,1/2$-inch lag screws. Drive the lag screws up through the top braces and into the top. Do *not* glue the table top to the braces.

8   Assemble the fence.   Sand the fence parts smooth and assemble them with glue. First glue the face to the base, and the dust collector top to the back. Let the glue set up, then glue the six relieved braces to the fence assembly and the two square braces to the dust collector assembly. Once again, let the glue set up. Finally, glue the dust collector to the fence. Let the glue dry completely, and sand all joints clean and flush.

Reinforce the glue joints with #8 x $1\,1/4$-inch flathead wood screws. Counterbore and countersink these screws so the heads are *at least* $1/4$ inch below the surface of the wood. *This is extremely important!* If the screws aren't sunk deep enough, you might nick them when you joint the fence. Cover the screw heads with wooden plugs, and sand the plugs flush with the wood surface.

9   Cut the mortise for the mounting plate.   The router mounting plate is mortised into the table top so the top of the plate will be flush with the work surface. Figure the size of the mounting plate, then rout a $3/4$-inch-wide, $3/8$-inch-deep square groove in the table. The outside dimensions of this groove must match the length and width of the mounting plate. (*SEE FIGURE 7-1.*)

After making the groove, cut out the waste in the middle of the mortise. There are several ways to do

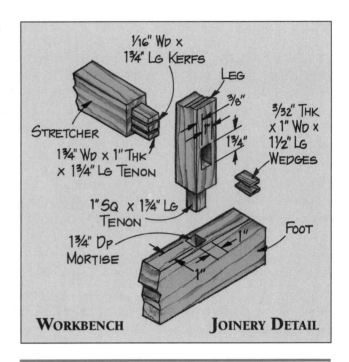

WORKBENCH   JOINERY DETAIL

this, but one of the easiest is to make a "plunge cut" with a circular saw. (*SEE FIGURE 7-2.*) This will turn the groove into a rabbet.

10   Make and install the router mounting plate.   Cut the mounting plate from $3/8$-inch-thick clear acrylic plastic, as shown in the *Mounting Plate Layout*. Round the corners to fit the plate to the mortise. Drill a hole in the middle of the plate, through which the router bits will protrude.

Use the router sole to mark the location of the $3/16$-inch-diameter mounting holes. Drill and countersink these holes. Also drill and countersink eight $3/16$-inch-diameter holes around the perimeter of the plate. Secure the mounting plate in the table with #8 x 1-inch flathead wood screws.

If you plan to do much freehand routing, drill a $1/4$-inch-diameter, 1-inch-deep hole near the righthand edge of the mounting plate, as shown in the *Workbench/Top View*. This hole will hold a "starting pin" to help you begin freehand cuts safely.

11   Cut the grooves for the miter gauge and the slots for the fence.   Carefully measure the width and thickness of your miter gauge bar. (Most are $3/4$ inch wide and $3/8$ inch thick.) Rout two slots across the router table, one on either side of the mounting plate, as shown in the *Workbench/Top View*. The slots should be the same dimensions as the bar.

Also rout four ³/₈-inch-wide, 10¹/₂-inch-long slots through the table top to mount the fence. Two of the slots should run front to back, and the other two side to side, as shown in the *Workbench/Top View*. Both pairs of slots must be precisely 19³/₄ inches center to center.

12 **Mount the fence.** Insert ³/₈ x 3-inch carriage bolts through the holes in the fence base and one of the pairs of slots. Secure the fence to the table with ³/₈-inch flat washers and wing nuts.

Using a square, check that the fence face is perpendicular to the work surface. With a straightedge, test the straightness of the fence face. If the fence is out of alignment, remove it from the router table and joint the face square to the base. (*See Figure 7-3.*)

13 **Finish the router table.** Remove the router mounting plate from the table. Lightly sand the table and the fence, making sure that all the surfaces are clean and all the joints are flush. Apply several coats of tung oil, letting each coat dry for 24 hours. Be sure to apply as many coats to the underside of the table top as you do the top side — this will help prevent the top from warping.

Rub out the finish with #0000 steel wool and paste wax. Buff the wax to a soft lustre. From time to time, apply a new coat of wax to the table top, the miter gauge slots, and the fence face. This will help the work slide smoothly across the table. When the table is finished and waxed, replace the mounting plate.

7-2 To remove the waste in the center of the mortise, make a plunge cut with a circular saw along each edge. Hold the saw above the table and place the nose of the saw base on the work surface. Turn on the saw and let the saw pivot on its nose so the blade slices into the table. Square the corners (where the circular saw blade won't reach) with a saber saw. As the waste falls away, the square groove will become a rabbet.

7-1 To make the mortise for the router mounting plate, first rout a square groove in the table top. Use a simple wooden frame to guide the router. Cut the groove in several passes, cutting just ¹/₈ inch deeper with each pass. Don't rout out the waste in the center of the mortise; leave it to help support the router as you work.

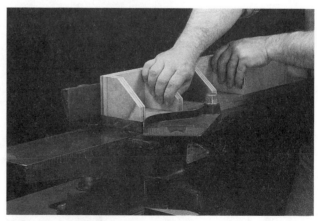

7-3 To ensure that the router table fence is straight and square, joint the face, keeping the base firmly against the jointer fence. Make very light cuts, and be careful not to cut into any of the screw heads.

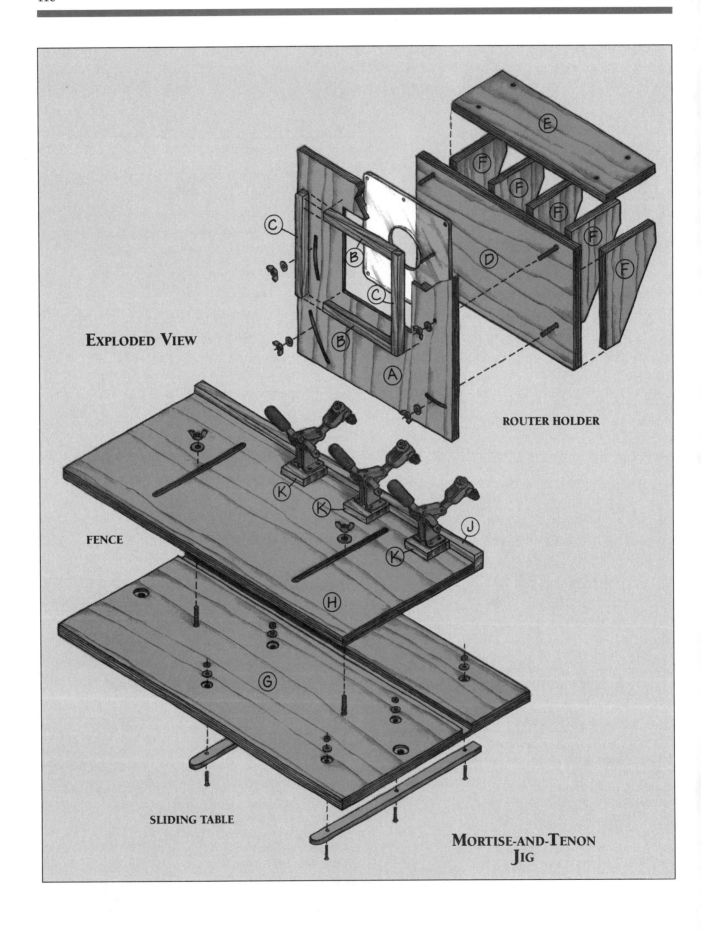

Exploded View

Router Holder

Fence

Sliding Table

Mortise-and-Tenon Jig

Mortise-and-Tenon Jig

Materials List (FINISHED DIMENSIONS)

Parts

A. Router
   holder   ³/₄″ x 18″ x 19½″

B. Reinforcing
   rails (2)   ³/₄″ x ³/₄″ x (variable)

C. Reinforcing
   stiles (2)   ³/₄″ x ³/₄″ x (variable)

D. Holder
   mount   ³/₄″ x 11½″ x 18″

E. Ledger   ³/₄″ x 5³/₄″ x 18″

F. Ledger
   braces (5)   ³/₄″ x 5³/₄″ x 9¼″

G. Mortise-and-tenon
   sliding table   ³/₄″ x 16″ x 25″

H. Mortise-and-tenon
   fence   ³/₄″ x 11¼″ x 25″

J. Fence face   ³/₄″ x 1¼″ x 25″

K. Clamp
   mounts (3)   ½″ x 2″ x 2″

Hardware

³/₈″ x 2″ Carriage bolts (4)

³/₈″ x 3″ Carriage bolts (2)

³/₈″ Flat washers (6)

³/₈″ Wing nuts (6)

³/₈″ Transparent acrylic plastic
sheet (size variable)

#8 x 1″ Flathead wood screws (8)

⁵/₈″ Flathead machine screws
(3) to fit router base

³/₈″ x ³/₄″ Acrylic plastic guide bars
(2 – optional)

³/₁₆″ x 1″ Flathead machine screws
(6 – optional)

³/₁₆″ Flat washers (6 – optional)

³/₁₆″ Hex nuts (6 – optional)

³/₈″ x 3″ Carriage bolts (2)

³/₈″ x 2″ Carriage bolts (2)

³/₈″ Flat washers (4)

³/₈″ Wing nuts (4)

Vertical toggle clamps (2–3)

#10 x ³/₄″ Panhead screws (8–12)

#10 x 1½″ Flathead wood screws
(24–30)

Plan of Procedure

1 Cut the parts. Cut the rails, stiles, face, and clamps mounts from hardwood. Make the remaining parts from cabinet-grade plywood.

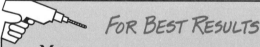

FOR BEST RESULTS

Make the mortise-and-tenon table from MDF (medium density fiberboard) or a laminate-covered sink cutout. A plywood table will work well, but plywood sometimes warps slightly. MDF and sink cutouts are more stable and remain flat.

2 Make and fit the router mounting plate.
Figure the size of the router mounting plate — you'll probably want to make it the same size as the plate in the router workbench. Cut an opening for the mounting plate in the holder, using the same method you used to make the opening in the workbench — rout a square groove, then cut out the waste. (You can even use the same wooden frame to guide the router.) Make

the mounting plate from transparent plastic, and fit it to the opening. Do not fasten it to the holder yet.

3 Drill the holes and cut the curved slots in the holder and mount. Stack the holder and the mount face to face, with the bottom and side edges flush. Stick the two parts together with double-faced carpet tape. On the mount, lay out the locations of the ³/₈-inch-diameter holes, as shown in the *Router Holder/ Back View*. Drill 1-inch-diameter, ³/₈-inch-deep counterbores for the top two holes, then drill all four holes through both the mount and the holder. Remove the mount from the holder and discard the tape.

Make an elongated sole for your router, as shown in the *Curved Slot Routing Jig,* from a scrap of ¼-inch plywood. Remove the sole from your router, mount a ³/₈-inch straight bit in the chuck, and attach the jig to the router base.

On the holder, mark where the curved slots should start and stop as shown in the *Router Holder/Front View.* Insert a ³/₈-inch carriage bolt through the hole at the small end of the jig and the hole in the upper right-

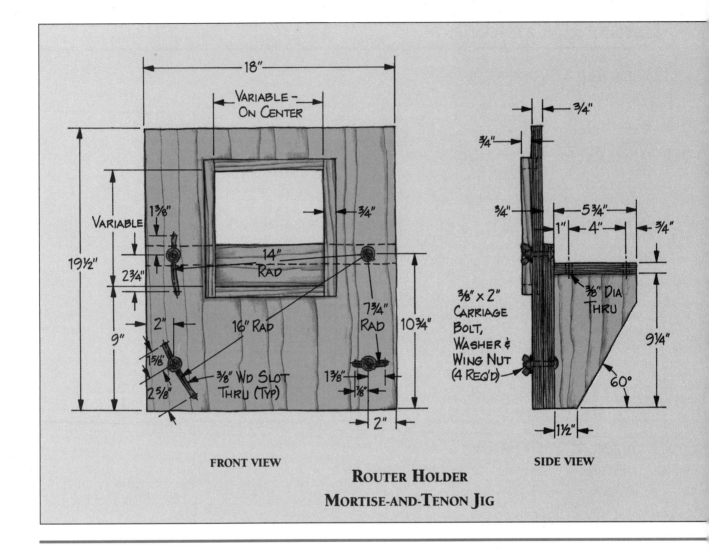

ROUTER HOLDER
MORTISE-AND-TENON JIG

hand corner of the mount. Rout the 16-inch-radius slot in several passes, using the bolt as a pivot. (*SEE FIGURE 7-4.*) Move the pivot bolt one hole closer to the router in the jig, but re-insert it in the same hole in the holder. Cut the 14-inch-radius slot. Repeat, and make the 7¾-inch-radius slot.

4 Install the mounting plate in the holder.
Glue the reinforcing rails and stiles to the holder. The inside edges of these parts should be flush with the inside edges of the router opening. Place the mounting plate in its mortise and attach it with #8 x 1-inch flathead wood screws. Remember — the heads of the screws must be countersunk so they're flush with or slightly below the surface of the plate.

5 Cut the shapes of the braces. Stack the braces face to face and stick them together with double-faced

carpet tape. All the ends and edges must be flush. Cut them diagonally with a band saw or handsaw, as shown in the *Router Holder/Side View.* Sand the sawed edges, disassemble, and discard the tape.

6 Assemble the mount, ledger, and braces.
Glue the mount, ledger, and braces together, reinforcing the glue joints with #10 x 1½-inch flathead wood screws. Countersink the heads of the screws. When the glue has dried, sand the joints clean and flush.

7 Attach the router holder to the workbench.
Clamp the mount assembly to your workbench so the outside face of the mount is flush with the outside edge of the workbench. Lay out the location of the ⅜-inch-diameter holes on the bench, as shown in the *Mortise-and-Tenon Jig/Workbench Layout.* Drill 1-inch-diameter, ¼-inch-deep counterbores at each

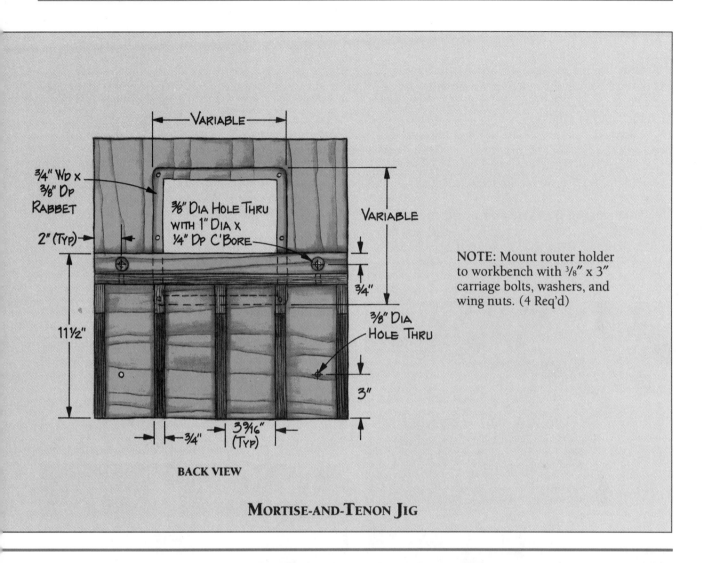

Variable

¾" Wd x
⅜" Dp
Rabbet

⅜" Dia Hole Thru
with 1" Dia x
¼" Dp C'Bore

2" (Typ)

Variable

¾"

⅜" Dia
Hole Thru

11½"

3"

NOTE: Mount router holder
to workbench with ⅜" x 3"
carriage bolts, washers, and
wing nuts. (4 Req'd)

¾"

3⁹⁄₁₆"
(Typ)

BACK VIEW

MORTISE-AND-TENON JIG

7-4 Make the curved slots in the
holder with a router and an elongated
sole. This sole will serve as a jig to
rout the curved slots. Insert a carriage bolt in the upper right-hand
hole in the holder and use it as the
pivot for all three slots.

mark, then drill ³/₈-inch-diameter holes through the bench *and* the mount assembly.

Remove the mount from the bench. Attach the holder assembly to the mount assembly with ³/₈ x 2-inch carriage bolts, flat washers, and wing nuts. Reattach the mount to the bench with ³/₈ x 3-inch carriage bolts, washers, and nuts. (The heads of the carriage bolts that rest in counterbores must be slightly below the work surface.) When you loosen the wing nuts, the holder should pivot on the mount. (*See Figure 7-5.*)

8 **Rout slots in the table and workbench (optional).** As shown, the sliding table travels back and forth in two ³/₄-inch-wide, ³/₈-inch-deep grooves cut into the workbench or router table. These grooves

are optional, as are the guide bars on the bottom of the sliding table. The purpose of the sliding table is to give you better control when routing small or slender workpieces. You can slide this table along the work surface, feeding the wood into the bit, with or without the grooves. Although the grooves will improve the accuracy of some operations, they aren't absolutely necessary.

If you decide you want the grooves, lay them out as shown in the *Mortise-and-Tenon Jig/Workbench Layout.* Cut them in several passes with a portable router and ³/₄-inch straight bit. (*See Figure 7-6.*)

9 **Cut the slots in the table and fence.** You must also rout several slots and grooves that are *not* optional:

■ A ³/₄-inch-wide, ³/₈-inch-deep miter gauge groove in the sliding table, as shown in the *Sliding Table/Top View*

■ ³/₈-inch-wide slots through the fence, as shown in the *Fence/Top View*

7-5 When fastened to its mount, the router holder pivots up and down several inches. This enables you to raise and lower the router. To lock the router at the desired height, tighten the wing nuts.

7-6 If you wish, rout grooves in the router workbench to guide the sliding table. Make each groove in several passes, using a straightedge to guide the router.

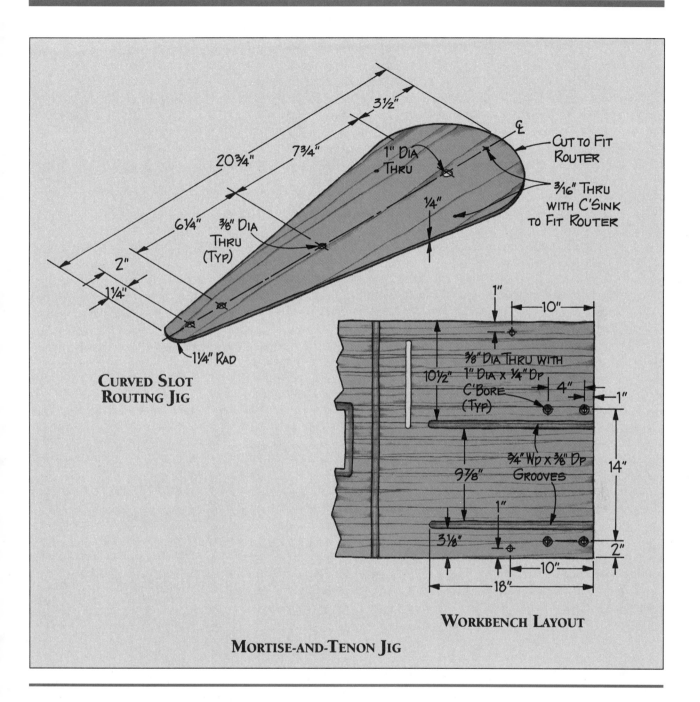

CURVED SLOT ROUTING JIG

WORKBENCH LAYOUT

MORTISE-AND-TENON JIG

10 **Drill holes in the sliding table and guide bars.** Lay out the locations of the four ³/₈-inch-diameter holes in the sliding table, as shown in the *Sliding Table/Top View*. Also mark the ¹/₄-inch-diameter holes, if you intend to mount the optional guide bars. Drill 1-inch-diameter, ¹/₄-inch-deep counterbores for the ³/₈-inch-diameter holes, and ³/₄-inch-diameter, ³/₈-inch-deep counterbores for the ¹/₄-inch-diameter holes.

Note: As shown in the drawings, drill the two 1-inch-diameter counterbores closest to the edges in the *top* side of the table, and the remaining two in the *bottom*.

Drill the two ³/₈-inch-diameter holes *farthest* from the edge through the table. Don't drill the other two yet.

Drill and countersink ³/₁₆-inch-diameter holes in the plastic guide bars, as shown in the *Sliding Table/End View*. These holes should be spaced precisely the same as the ¹/₄-inch-diameter holes in the table.

Fasten the guide bars to the sliding table with ³/₁₆ x 1-inch flathead machine screws, flat washers, and hex

(continued) ▷

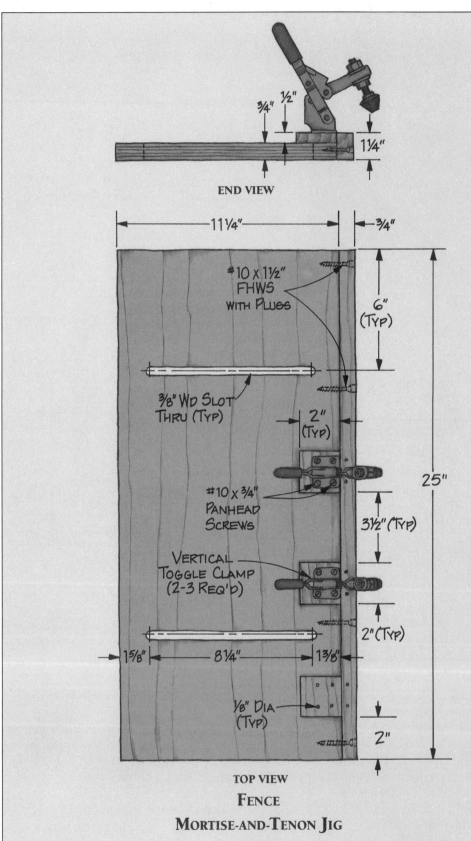

END VIEW

#10 x 1½"
FHWS
WITH PLUGS

11¼"   ¾"

¾" ½"

1¼"

6"
(TYP)

⅜" WD SLOT
THRU (TYP)

2"
(TYP)

#10 x ¾"
PANHEAD
SCREWS

25"

VERTICAL
TOGGLE CLAMP
(2-3 REQ'D)

3½" (TYP)

2" (TYP)

1⅝"   8¼"   1⅜"

⅛" DIA
(TYP)

2"

TOP VIEW
FENCE
MORTISE-AND-TENON JIG

NOTE: For mortising operations, secure fence to sliding
table with ⅜" x 2" carriage
bolts, washers, and wing nuts.
(2 Sets Req'd)

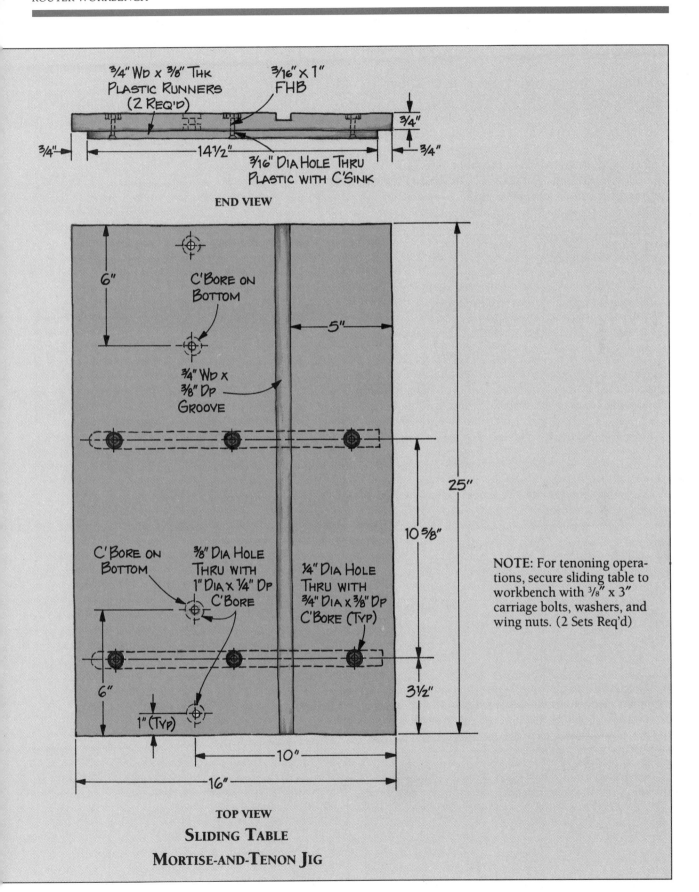

END VIEW

TOP VIEW

SLIDING TABLE

MORTISE-AND-TENON JIG

NOTE: For tenoning operations, secure sliding table to workbench with ³/₈" x 3" carriage bolts, washers, and wing nuts. (2 Sets Req'd)

nuts, but do *not* tighten the nuts yet. Place the sliding table on the workbench or router table, fitting the guide bars in their grooves. Position the table so the outside edge is flush with the outside edge of the bench. (Because the bolt holes in the sliding table are slightly oversize, you will be able to shift it slightly.) When the edges are flush, tighten the hex nuts.

Check the sliding action of the table. If it's difficult to move at any point, you may have to loosen the hex nuts and realign one of the bars.

Try This Trick

To help the table slide smoothly, wax *and* buff the bench surface, the underside of the table, the guide bars, and the grooves.

When the table slides freely, reposition it so the edges of the table and the bench are flush. Clamp the table to the bench so it can't move, and drill the two remaining ³/₈-inch-diameter holes down through the sliding table *and* the workbench. (*See Figure 7-7.*)

11   Attach the face to the fence.   Glue the face to the fence. Reinforce the glue joint with #10 x 1¹/₂-inch flathead wood screws. Counterbore *and* countersink the screws so the heads are at least ¹/₄ inch below the surface. Cover the screw heads with plugs, let the glue dry, then sand the plugs flush with the wood surface.

Joint the face, making sure the surface is straight and true. Be careful not to cut into the heads of the screws.

12   Install the clamps.   Glue the clamp blocks to the fence, just behind the face, as shown in the *Fence/ Top View*. Drill ¹/₈-inch-diameter mounting holes in the blocks and top edge of the face. Attach the clamps with #10 x ³/₄-inch panhead screws.

Try This Trick

Drill several pairs of holes so you can move the clamps forward and back as needed.

---

13   Attach the fence to the table.   Insert ³/₈ x 2-inch carriage bolts up through the two ³/₈-inch-diameter inside holes in the sliding table. Lay the fence on the table so the bolts protrude up through the grooves. Secure the fence to the table with flat washers and wing nuts.

7-7   With the sliding table clamped to the workbench, drill bolt holes through *both* the table and the bench. This will enable you to secure the table to the bench for tenoning and other operations in which you don't want the table to slide.

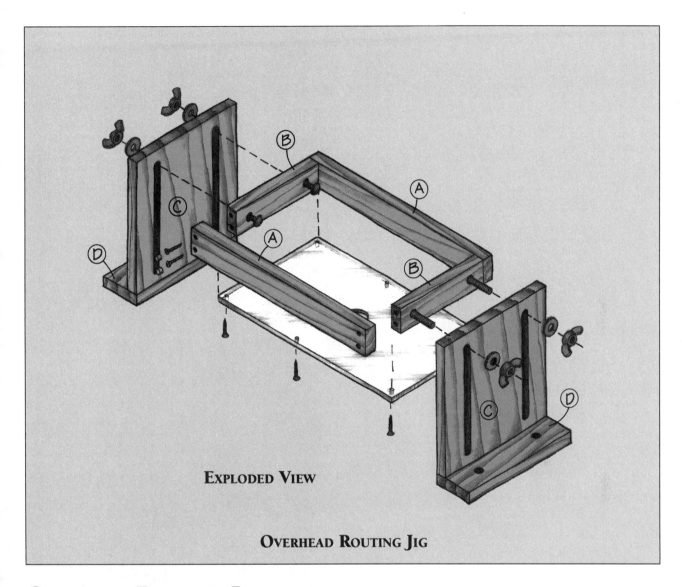

EXPLODED VIEW

OVERHEAD ROUTING JIG

OVERHEAD ROUTING JIG

MATERIALS LIST (FINISHED DIMENSIONS)

Parts

A. Platform
   sides (2) $3/4'' \times 2'' \times 16''$
B. Platform
   ends (2) $3/4'' \times 2'' \times$ (variable)
C. Platform supports
   (2) $3/4'' \times$ (variable) $\times 10''$
D. Platform
   feet (2) $3/4'' \times 3'' \times$ (variable)

Hardware

$3/8'' \times$ (variable) $\times 16''$ Transparent
   acrylic plastic sheet
#10 x $1^{1}/4''$ Flathead wood screws
   (14)
#8 x 1" Flathead wood screws (10)
$3/8'' \times 2''$ Carriage bolts (4)
$3/8'' \times 3''$ Carriage bolts (4)
$3/8''$ Flat washers (8)
$3/8''$ Wing nuts (8)
$5/8''$ lg. Flathead machine screws
   (3) to fit router base

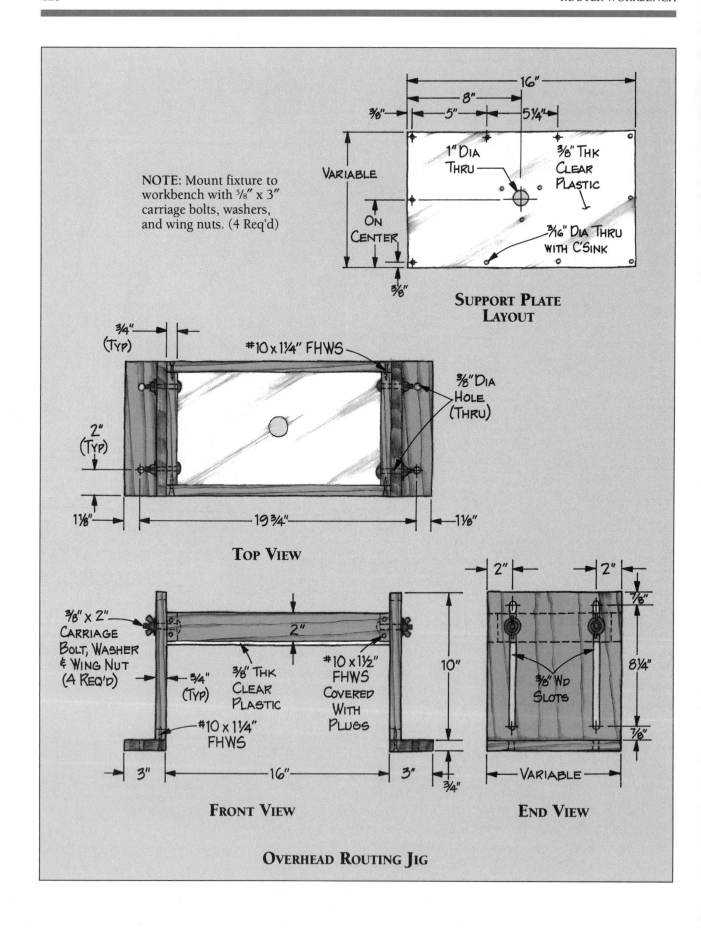

NOTE: Mount fixture to workbench with ⅝" x 3" carriage bolts, washers, and wing nuts. (4 Req'd)

SUPPORT PLATE LAYOUT

TOP VIEW

FRONT VIEW

END VIEW

OVERHEAD ROUTING JIG

PLAN OF PROCEDURE

1 Figure the size of the jig and cut the parts.
Determine the width of the jig — the distance between the inside faces of the platform sides should be just a little more than the diameter of your router. From this, calculate the length of the platform ends and feet, and the width of the supports.

You may also want to adjust other dimensions. For example, depending on the work you have to do, you may need to hold the router higher than shown. If so, lengthen the supports. If you lengthen them beyond 16 inches, lengthen the feet 1 to 2 inches, too. Add braces between the feet and the supports to keep the fixture steady.

Or you may want to make the platform longer to have more working space beneath it. (This is especially important when pin-routing.) To do this, simply lengthen the platform sides. However, you should also make both the sides and the ends wider — this will prevent the platform from flexing in the middle.

Consider these possibilities and adjust the dimensions as necessary. Then cut the parts from solid hardwood.

2 Drill the platform ends and feet. Drill ³/₈-inch-diameter holes through the platform ends, as shown in the *Top View.* Also drill holes through the feet.

3 Cut the slots in the supports. Lay out the slots on the supports, as shown in the *End View.* Double-check your layout by placing a platform end on top of each support — the bolt holes must line up with the slots. Cut the slots with a table-mounted router and a ³/₈-inch straight bit.

4 Assemble the platform and supports. Glue the platform sides to the ends, and the feet to the supports. Reinforce the glue joints with #10 x 1¹/₄-inch flathead wood screws, countersinking the screws so the heads are flush or slightly below the surface. Let the glue dry, then sand the joints clean and flush.

5 Make and install the support plate. Cut the support plate from transparent plastic — it should be the same width and length as the platform. (Although, if the platform is exceptionally long, the plate doesn't need to run the full length.) In this plate, drill several holes:
- A 1-inch-diameter hole for the bit, through the

center, as shown in the *Support Plate Layout,* through which the bit will protrude
- Appropriate size holes with countersinks to mount the router — use the sole as a template to mark the locations
- ³/₁₆-inch-diameter holes with countersinks around the perimeter of the plate

Attach the plate to the underside of the platform with #8 x 1-inch flathead wood screws.

6 Assemble the jig. Insert ³/₈ x 2-inch carriage bolts through the holes in the platform ends. Fit the slotted supports over the bolts, and check the sliding action. The platform should slide up and down without binding. If it binds, file away a little stock from inside the slots. When the platform slides smoothly, secure the legs with flat washers and wing nuts.

VARIATIONS

To make your router workbench even more useful, you may wish to add some storage units under the work surface. Shown is one possible arrangement of drawers and cupboards.

INDEX

Note: Page references in *italic* indicate photographs or illustrations.
Boldface references indicate charts or tables.

WOODWORKING GLOSSARY

TENON DETAIL

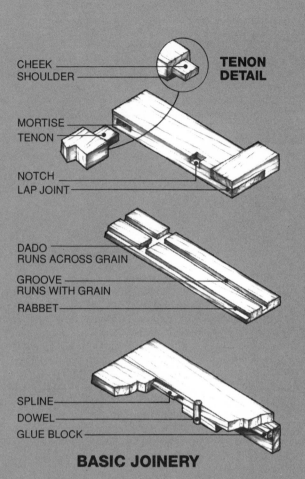

CHEEK
SHOULDER

MORTISE
TENON

NOTCH
LAP JOINT

BASIC JOINERY

DADO
RUNS ACROSS GRAIN

GROOVE
RUNS WITH GRAIN

RABBET

SPLINE
DOWEL
GLUE BLOCK

FINGER JOINT

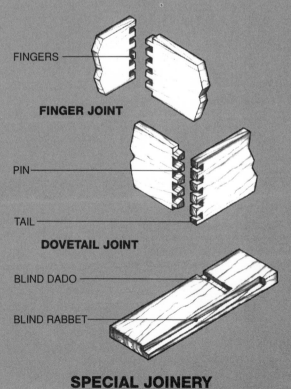

FINGERS

DOVETAIL JOINT

PIN

TAIL

SPECIAL JOINERY

BLIND DADO

BLIND RABBET

COMMON SHAPES

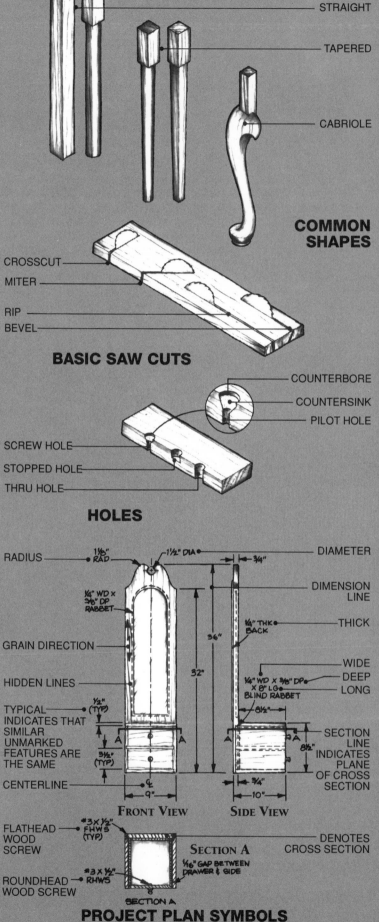

STRAIGHT

TAPERED

CABRIOLE

BASIC SAW CUTS

CROSSCUT

MITER

RIP

BEVEL

HOLES

COUNTERBORE

COUNTERSINK

PILOT HOLE

SCREW HOLE

STOPPED HOLE

THRU HOLE

PROJECT PLAN SYMBOLS

RADIUS — 1⅛" RAD

1½" DIA — DIAMETER

¾"

¼" WD x ³⁄₈" DP RABBET

DIMENSION LINE

¼" THK BACK — THICK

36"

32"

¼" WD x ³⁄₈" DP X 8" LG BLIND RABBET

WIDE
DEEP
LONG

GRAIN DIRECTION

HIDDEN LINES

TYPICAL INDICATES THAT SIMILAR UNMARKED FEATURES ARE THE SAME

½" (TYP)

3½" (TYP)

8½"

8½"

SECTION LINE INDICATES PLANE OF CROSS SECTION

CENTERLINE

¢

9"

¾"

10"

FRONT VIEW

SIDE VIEW

FLATHEAD WOOD SCREW

#3 X ½" FHWS (TYP)

SECTION A

⅟₁₆" GAP BETWEEN DRAWER & GIDE

DENOTES CROSS SECTION

ROUNDHEAD WOOD SCREW

#3 X ½" RHWS

SECTION A